PRAISE FOR *CYBER MAYDAY AND THE DAY AFTER*

"This is the first practical book on cybersecurity I could not put down – it wouldn't let me. It is filled with easily relatable true stories and facts. It's exceptionally well-written and engaging, and nearly every page contains a gem of practical advice. This work is simply indispensable for all public managers to read, absorb, and act. Lohrmann's and Tan's front-line cyber experience brings years of collective wisdom together into one wonderful fact-filled book that one will treasure and will want to always have by their side."

> Dr. Alan R. Shark, Executive Director of CompTIA's Public Technology Institute (PTI)

"Most leaders I speak with have 'cybercrime headlines' fatigue. We all need a guidebook and to know we are not alone. A must-read on every leader's list is the collaborative book project by Dan and Shamane; they hit it out of the park with *Cyber Mayday and the Day After*! This is an extraordinary book, brilliantly put together for today's leaders as our modern world of cyberattacks does not discriminate between businesses and individuals. They have done a splendid job in storytelling and capturing battlefront lessons, revealing degrees of knowledge and wisdom in such a riveting way.

"If you are in the cybersecurity industry, a business leader, or an executive, this is *the* book you should read next. Readers will walk away with insights and knowledge gathered from behind the scenes. They summarize their findings in an effective guide to preparing, managing, and responding to future cyber maydays."

> Theresa Payton, The White House's first female CIO, author of *Manipulated*, CEO of Fortalice Solutions

"Cyber Mayday and the Day After is a book that everyone who cares about the survivability of their business should read. The insights and suggested approaches to the vast problem we face in setting up our defenses and better responding to cyberthreats in this book are top-notch. The authors have made a complex problem clear and easy to understand and have based their guidance on methods that make a difference. To be blunt, read this book now!"

Dr. Chase Cunnnigham, cybersecurity expert, known as "Dr. Zero Trust," author of *Cyber Warfare—Truth, Tactics, and Strategies* and the new novel *gAbrIel*

"In my long career in cybersecurity, I have read and written about incident response, what it is, and why CISOs and their businesses should care. In *Cyber Mayday and the Day After* authors Daniel Lohrmann and Shamane Tan take it a step further and provide an exceptional guide on how businesses today can prepare and survive an incident. It is well-written with excellent insight into what it takes for security and business leaders to be resilient. I really enjoyed the chance to read this book and believe it will be an excellent resource for our community."

Gary Hayslip, CISO of Softbank Investment Advisors

"As organizations face the continual onslaught of cyberattacks, leaders need a practical guide to understand where to start, how to prioritize, and what to do when the inevitable breach occurs. The amount of data available today describing what leaders can and should do is overwhelming. *Cyber Mayday and the Day After* provides a roadmap with specific examples, where leaders can learn from their peers and chart a course that fits their organizations to ensure that they are prepared for today and tomorrow. The book is a must-read for business and government CIOs, CISOs, and other government leaders."

Teri Takai, Executive Director of the Center for Digital Government, former CIO for the U.S. Department of Defense (DoD), and former CIO for the states of California and Michigan

"Dan Lohrmann and Shamane Tan have written a truly important book on what to do when cyber calamity inevitably strikes. It is both an extensive resource and an operating manual for anyone in cybersecurity leadership roles (plus anyone connected online). With the growing digital ecosystem of billions of devices and sensors, we are all potential (and likely) targets of sophisticated hackers abetted by automated technologies searching for cyber vulnerabilities. Their book provides strategies and plans for gap analysis, incident response, and especially resilience. Disruptive breaches are going to happen no matter what. Reading and keeping *Cyber Mayday and the Day After: A Leader's Guide to Preparing, Managing, and Recovering from the Inevitable* as a ready reference is indispensable."

Chuck Brooks, President of Brooks Consulting International, Georgetown University Adjunct Professor, Named Top Tech Person to Follow by LinkedIn

"Loved the book! In a world of never-ending 'shock' statistics and cyber doom mongering, Shamane and Dan combine the power of storytelling and practical checklists in a refreshing way to help cyber and risk management professionals increase their cyber resilience. Read the airport data leakage or CISO hire-gone-wrong examples in Chapter 1 and ask yourself, 'Could that be my company?' If so, I highly recommend that you read the rest of the book. Learn from it. Apply the many resilience blueprints. And then share it with someone you care about.

Written in their usual engaging and deceptively simple style, *Cyber Mayday and the Day After* is an invaluable reference guide for today's cyber risk management community."

Ellie Warner, Global Head, Training and Awareness, Trust Data and Resilience, Standard Chartered Bank

"Writing a book on cybersecurity is a tricky business. It could dive into low-level technical details or float too high, proffering overly general advice, either way losing the reader. A practicing or aspiring CISO is looking for pointers to prevent, manage, and recover from cyber incidents. This book, organized in three sections of pre-attack preparation, on-attack actions, and post-attack recovery, hits the sweet spot by driving home the points through context-appropriate case studies presented in lively prose. The case studies presented by the authors, mostly from recent times, offer a rich trove of knowledge for any security practitioner. The authors have taken the extra step of interviewing the CISOs in these case studies and brought out subtle nuances of their thought processes and how they execute their actions. This easy-reading book is a must in every security practitioner's bookshelf."

Dr. Siva Sivasubramanian, Chief Information Security Officer,
Singtel Optus

CYBER
MAYDAY

AND THE DAY AFTER

CYBER MAYDAY

AND THE DAY AFTER

A LEADER'S GUIDE TO
PREPARING, MANAGING, AND RECOVERING
FROM INEVITABLE BUSINESS DISRUPTIONS

DAN LOHRMANN AND SHAMANE TAN

WILEY

Library of Congress Cataloging-in-Publication Data is Available:

ISBN: 978-1-119-83530-1 (Hardback)
ISBN: 978-1-119-83532-5 (ePDF)
ISBN: 978-1-119-83531-8 (ePub)

COVER DESIGN: PAUL MCCARTHY
COVER ART: GETTY IMAGES:
AERIALPERSPECTIVE IMAGES / JOSE A. BERNAT BACETE

SKY10030296_100121

Contents

Introduction: Setting the Global Stage for Cyber Resilience

We worried for decades about WMDs – weapons of mass destruction. Now it is time to worry about a new kind of WMDs – weapons of mass disruption.

–John Mariotti

Tuesday, May 1, 2035

Something was not right.

As Julie stood by the front door of her parents' home in Park Ridge, Illinois, her A-ride (slang for autonomous transportation) was nowhere in sight. She was going to be late for work. "My new boss is going to be furious," she inwardly panicked.

This was the one day a month that she actually was required to be downtown for a team meeting, and her 7:15 a.m. FastUber pickup (with nonstop express service to the Chicago Loop) was nowhere to be found. And FastUbers are never late.

"Miranda – where is my ride? What's going on? Where are all the cars?"

Strange, no response from her automated assistant, which usually answered her questions before she even finished her sentences. Julie momentarily thought about her grandmother as she peered angrily at the small speaker over her glasses. She briefly smiled when she thought about how she nicknamed her personal assistant Miranda, in memory of her grandmother.

"Now I'm pissed! I even paid extra for express today." As Julie noticed that both the children across the street and Mr. Stevens next door were also waiting for their rides, she realized something else must be happening. A new emotion overcame her – fear.

Julie went back in the house and shouted at the wall. "NEWS!"

A holographic image of CNN lit up the room, showing two reporters standing under a chyron reading: "BREAKING NEWS." An artificial intelligence voice announced: "Widespread impact is simultaneously hitting global airports, Wall Street firms, international banks, the London Underground, Australian ports, and thousands of educational learning centers."

Julie posed her question to the hologram: "Do you believe this may be a nation-state attack?"

A reporter standing in front of New York's One World Trade Center responded: "That's certainly a likely possibility. Mass transit has stopped, banks are down, some cities are experiencing power outages, hospitals are on emergency generators, school technology is down, universities have canceled classes, and, most shocking of all – trading floors from London to New York to Chicago are now closed.

"Hold on a moment, please, we are receiving word that the president of the United States has just declared a Nationwide Cyber Emergency, under the authority of the Cyber Disruption Act of 2028."

A NEW SENSE OF CYBER URGENCY

While this 2035 Mayday scenario is just fiction, the bombardment of daily security incidents is beyond eye-opening in real life. With the ongoing digital transformation, which accelerated even faster in diverse areas of society and every corner of the globe during the COVID-19 pandemic, the impact of cyber emergency incidents has been felt from hospitals to high schools, from elections to electric grids, from main street retailers to Wall Street bankers, and from small-town PTA meetings to United Nations Security Council meetings.

The following quotes are very real, coming after an unprecedented barrage of cyberattacks hit global governments and businesses in 2020 and 2021:

> **President Joe Biden:** "We've elevated the status of cyber issues within our government," President Biden said in a national security speech at the State Department. "We are launching an urgent initiative to improve our capability, readiness, and resilience in cyberspace."[1]

> **U.S. Federal Reserve Chairman Jerome Powell:** When we talk about cyber risk, what kind of scenarios are we looking at? U.S. Federal Reserve chairman Jerome Powell responded to host Scott Pelley, as part of a *60 Minutes* interview, "All different kinds. I mean, there are scenarios in which a large payment utility, for example, breaks down and the payment system can't work. Payments can't be completed. There are scenarios in which a large financial institution would lose the ability to track the payments that it's making and things like that. Things like that where you would have a part of the financial system come to a halt, or perhaps even a broad part."

> Powell continued: "And so we spend so much time and energy and money guarding against these things. There are cyber attacks every day on all major institutions now. And the government is working hard on that. So are all the private sector companies. There's a lot of effort going in to deal with those threats. That's a big part of the threat picture in today's world."

> Pelley: "How have we gotten away with not having a disaster like that?"

> Powell: "You know, I don't want to jinx us. I would just say we've worked very hard at it. A lot of us have worked very hard at this and invested a lot of time and money and thought. And worked collaboratively [*sic*] with our allies and with other government agencies. But there's never a feeling at any time that you've done enough or that you feel safe."[2]

FireEye CEO Kevin Mandia during U.S. Senate testimony on the Solarwinds breach: "Early in our investigation, we uncovered some tell-tale signs that the attackers were likely working for and trained by a foreign intelligence service. We were able to discover and identify these signs in reliance upon our catalog of the trace evidence of thousands of computer intrusion investigations conducted over the last 17 years. We record the digital fingerprints of every investigation we have undertaken with great rigor and discipline, and we are often able to use this catalog of evidence in order to attribute the threat actors in many of the incidents we respond to.

"Based on the knowledge gained through our years of experience responding to cyber incidents, we concluded that we were witnessing an attack by a nation with top-tier offensive capabilities. This attack was different from the multitude of incidents to which we have responded throughout the years. The attackers tailored their capabilities specifically to target and attack our company (and their other victims). They operated clandestinely, using methods that counter security tools and forensic examination. They also operated with both constraint and focus, targeting specific information and specific people, as if following collection requirements. They did not perform actions that were indiscriminate, and they did not appear to go on 'fishing expeditions.'

"Such focused targeting, combined with the novel combination of techniques not witnessed by us or our partners in the past, contributed to our conclusion that this was a foreign intelligence actor. Therefore, on December 8, 2020, we publicly disclosed that we were attacked by a highly sophisticated threat actor – one whose discipline, operational security, and techniques led us to believe it was a state-sponsored attack utilizing novel techniques. . . ."[3]

Microsoft president Brad Smith: "The Russians did not just want to get inside the houses of the victims. They wanted to find the most interesting valuables, which to them meant reading, examining, and in some cases taking data and information. Just as they used many ways to initially attack their victims and open a back door, they also used a variety of ways to compromise identity.

"It is important to understand this aspect of the attack: Unlike some attacks that take advantage of vulnerabilities in software, this attack was based on finding and stealing the privileges, certificates, tokens or other keys within on-premises networks (which together is referred to as 'identity') that would provide access to information in the same way the owner would access it. This approach was made much easier in networks where basic cybersecurity hygiene was not being observed – that is, where the keys to the safe and the car were left out in the open."[4]

SolarWinds CEO Sudhakar Ramakrishna: "We believe that the entire software industry should be concerned about the nation state attack as the methodologies and approaches that the threat actor(s) used can be replicated to impact software and hardware products from any company, and these are not SolarWinds-specific vulnerabilities.

"To this end, we are sharing our findings with the broader community of vendors, partners, and users so that together, we ensure the safety of our environments."[5]

Federal chief information security officer Christopher J. DeRusha: "We are at a crossroads for the nation's cybersecurity. The SolarWinds incident exposed gaps in our cybersecurity capabilities and risk management programs, not just in the federal government, but in some of the most mature and well-resourced companies in the world. This event should serve as both a wakeup call and a galvanizing opportunity for the federal government and industry to come together and tackle these threats with renewed resolve. This collaboration is critical, as private-sector entities have primary responsibility for the defense and security of their networks. The government must communicate threat assessments to inform private-sector security operations and ensure common situational awareness.

"This incident comes amid a series of aggressive and high-profile attacks on federal systems, attempted theft of the data used to develop the COVID-19 vaccines, ransomware attacks on U.S. hospitals, and new technology and security challenges that arose with the rapid shift to remote work. These myriad challenges underscore the importance and urgency of modernizing federal IT and strengthening U.S. cybersecurity capabilities."[6]

U.S. Senator Ben Sasse (R-Neb.) after a critical U.S. fuel pipeline system was shut down by a cyberattack in early May 2021: "There's obviously much still to learn about how this attack happened, but we can be sure of two things: This is a play that will be run again, and we're not adequately prepared. If Congress is serious about an infrastructure package, at front and center should be the hardening of these critical sectors."

Australian prime minister Scott Morrison: "Based on advice provided to me by our cyber experts, Australian organizations are currently being targeted by a sophisticated state-based cyber actor.

"This activity is targeting Australian organizations across a range of sectors, including all levels of government, industry, political organizations, education, health, central service providers, and operators of other critical infrastructure."[7]

A PEEK BEHIND THE CURTAINS, AND THE MAKING OF *CYBER MAYDAY AND THE DAY AFTER*

So why did we write this book?

First, we are passionate about cybersecurity. We love to share true stories and cybersecurity challenges and solutions in numerous ways, including our books, blogs, magazine articles, social media, global speeches, podcasts, and more.

Second, we believe that our unique backgrounds, experiences, and cultures offer a powerful combination of award-winning cybersecurity leadership experiences, partnerships, and stories. This book is intended for a global audience; in addition to a rich resource of insights brought in from around the world, Dan brings a U.S. perspective, while Shamane lives in Australia and works extensively throughout the Asia-Pacific region.

Third, this is a vital topic for the world at this time. The earlier quotes make that abundantly clear.

Fourth, other materials on this cyber topic tend to cover cyber incident response, cybersecurity emergency planning, cyber exercises, and related people/process/technology materials from one of two approaches. Some take an academic approach and offer checklists and detailed frameworks, such as walking the reader through the implementation of the five-function NIST Cybersecurity Framework: identify, protect, detect, respond, and recover. Other materials offer ad hoc stories and fun facts about statistics and costs associated with data breaches, ransomware, and a long list of other security incidents.

While we reference many of these works at the end of the book and point readers to helpful resources throughout, our goals are to bring cyber incident response and the associated planning, response, and recovery to life with true stories that offer compelling lessons and provide practical, actionable advice from leading global technology and security leaders and business executives who have been through the storm. We want to provide CxOs, directors, managers, technology professionals, and frontline business people with the tools they need to prepare for inevitable security incidents.

Bottom line, we offer powerful stories that motivate, along with cyber plans and free resources with practical steps that can be taken from small businesses to large enterprises in the public and private sectors. The goal: cyber resilience that will prepare your team and get you through most cybersecurity challenges you will likely face.

THE THREE-PART BREAKDOWN

The book is presented in three parts: Part I: A Leader's Guide to Preparing for the Inevitable; Part II: Cyber Mayday: When the Alarm Goes Off; and Part III: The Day After: Recovering from Cyber Emergencies.

Part I presents the gift of a time machine, seeking hindsight from top industry leaders around the globe and things we can do differently before having to go through any cyber emergencies. We cover playbooks from cyber disruption to risk transfer options, and explore the power of "perfect practice." We also unpack a handbook specifically for leaders at the top, and the keys of proactive leadership.

Part II is when Cyber Mayday hits! We walk through real-life cyber emergency incidents and what actually happens when the alarm goes off. In that split second when the virtual walls are crumbling down, what are the most important steps to take and where to go? Who are the players you should be working with in times of crisis and immense pressure? And, in the midst of your Mayday, what can go right?

The chapters in Part III address critical issues when you finally have some breathing space. This is the opportune time to be intentional and reflect on what went wrong, how to recover, and how to level up in your strategy.

This comprehensive exploration of tales, woes, and lessons of leaders is a gift of hindsight and insights, which will enable and position current and next-generation business leaders with the required foresight to continue leading at the frontline. We hope you gain lots of invaluable takeaways from your time spent with us; enjoy.

A Leader's Guide to Preparing for the Inevitable

CHAPTER 1

If I Had a Time Machine

The real trick in life is to turn hindsight into foresight that reveals insight.

—Robin Sharma

Imagine going back in time to watch and listen and change things. Where would you go? And to what point in time?

Do you have the knowledge, tools, and influence to change things for the better? If so, who would you interact with to alter the specific outcome(s)? What one (or perhaps two or three) things would you do differently, and why?

Yes, you can ponder these questions about virtually any area of life. However, this book specifically addresses cybersecurity incidents or other emergency situations that contain significant cyber components that have in the past, or are in the present, or will in the future, impact global organizations in substantial ways.

Stretching further, society is growing even more reliant on resilient infrastructures that demand functioning cyber protections that involve people, process, and technology components. If we fail, the consequences will be dramatic in real life.

This journey must start with the lessons from the past. We can learn from stories from global cyber leaders and practitioners who have been through cyberattacks and come out stronger. Along the way, we will

3

point to frameworks, checklists, standards, protocols, white papers, and other helpful materials.

If we are going to be equipped for the inevitable cyber storms that are coming in the decades ahead, we must learn from each other and improve faster than the bad actors who are causing such online destruction. In doing so, we first explore what works and is repeatable regarding cyber incident response.

STARTING WITH THE UNKNOWNS – OR NOT?

"I don't want to know, and I don't care to know. If I don't know about it, it does not exist." Shocking, but in fact, there are many business leaders who think this way.

The truth is that sometimes, some data takes only a minimal effort to discover, and when you realize the type of information that is available out there and accessible to anyone (including malicious actors), then you will have no choice but to care. As the chief growth officer at Privasec (*a Sekuro company*), a top-tier and agnostic cybersecurity firm, Shamane leads the security outreach strategy team, spearheading industry awareness initiatives while working closely with the CISOs (chief information security officers) in bridging their business gaps. She met Todd Carroll, a former 20-year FBI cyber intelligence leader, virtually, in a cyber security summit she organized, where he shared an intriguing story. Todd walked through one of the real-world findings that CybelAngel's data leak detection technology came across a few years ago.[1] CybelAngel detects exposed data, devices, and services outside the enterprise's perimeter, enabling remediation before the exposure is weaponized. In this instance, it detected several pieces of information that exposed a bigger issue involving several airports, their ecosystem, and exposure of their data.

The thing is, data is always being shared. The aviation industry, like other industries, works with third parties. The moment any organization shares information with a third party, it loses visibility or control over what is done with the data, despite their best efforts or intentions.

In this case, when CybelAngel performed a search and monitoring on keywords related to airport security, they detected nearly 10,000 servers that were publicly available, on which over 400 blueprints of airports worldwide were identified, sitting on unprotected third-party connected devices, or in misconfigured cloud storage.

Some of these blueprints were extremely detailed, including the location and angle of the security cameras, revealing which were motion activated or had facial recognition capabilities and even precise information on how to access and take control of them. In addition, these blueprints contained the location of the detention rooms that are hidden from the public, runways, and the position of the fuel lines from the tanks leading to the runway where fuel is pumped into the wings of the aircraft.

There were blank signed templates of security application access forms that, if compromised, would have allowed access into the airport facilities. There were also completed security badge application forms with official stamps and signatures, and over 300 files describing safety procedures and policies. Those procedures included instructions on how to bypass the whole security system, and how to deactivate it.

There were also identity details of air marshals and departure and arrival dates, as well as the list of weapons they are allowed to carry on planes. Such intricate information can easily serve as a blueprint for a terrorist attack.

The frightening part of all of this is that the data was found on third-party servers in many countries, including the United States, France, the UK, India, Spain, and others.

It was fortunate that the findings were reported to the impacted organizations in time and the FBI and Interpol worked on closing the thousands of open servers around the globe. Imagine the terrorism disaster that could have occurred had this information not been discovered due to a lack of interest and blind obliviousness.

As the world continues establishing even more interconnectivity, it becomes more critical than ever to position industry leaders to have better foresight before a crisis even happens.

AN ISOLATED PERSPECTIVE HAS MANY LIMITS

John Yates, QPM, is a former assistant commissioner in the London Metropolitan Police Service. He retired in November 2011 after a 30-year career. In his last role, John was the UK lead for counterterrorism and the most senior advisor to the prime minister and home secretary on law enforcement issues relating to terrorism. In this role he was also responsible for protecting the royal family and senior government ministers as well as the Houses of Parliament and Heathrow Airport.

John is currently the director of security for Scentre Group, which owns and operates Westfield Shopping Centres in Australia and New Zealand. He shared his lessons for the cyber industry from his counterterrorism days:

"One of the key roles of leaders is to keep out of the weeds and be constantly looking up, thinking broadly and identifying trends. I want to talk about a relatively little known case in London in 2010. It was a case that should have been examined in much more detail because it was one of the principal precursors to a deadly and murderous shift – the radicalization of predominantly young people – that plagued the efforts of those seeking to counter terrorism for many years and, indeed, continues to do so."

In a time where radicalization was little understood, particularly by young vulnerable people, Roshonara Choudhry, a final-year student at King's College, London, and from a good Bangladeshi family, brought two knives to Beckton Globe Library, where MP Stephen Timms was conducting his constituency clinic. Choudhry stabbed Timms twice in his abdomen.

"She missed his life organs by two millimeters. He nearly died." John further explained that Timms was the most popular MP in the country at that time, and he represented a community with a large population of Muslim residents. Yet Choudhry targeted him because he voted for the Iraq war. Despite Timms's work in the community, Choudhry had been radicalized online.

John continued, "This case was initially dealt with by the local homicide squad. It took us over 24 hours to realize that this was in fact a terrorist attack, being that it clearly fit the long accepted definition – the unlawful use of violence and intimidation for political or ideological aims.

"It was actually the first successful terrorist attack in London since the July bombings in 2005. So at the time, the case was taken over by the counterterrorism command and Choudhry was convicted and sentenced to life imprisonment.

"But we stopped there. For two years, we didn't really do anything, and then suddenly the whole problem of people being radicalized began to play out in developed countries, particularly in the Western world. ISIS emerged and the online community became an effective vector to radicalize people.

"What happened in 2010 was a significant event. What we failed to do was to identify the broader implications – that Al Qaeda and, later, ISIS were using social media and other online means to target vulnerable people – and pose the question, could this happen again and what should we be doing about it now?

"One of the duties of leaders is to take any extraordinary or unusual events and reflect on the underlying issues, to consider what the themes are that need to be addressed. Is there something that we need to be doing here in the education environment? Is there something that we should consider about the public warnings?

"We didn't do any of that for a number of years and then we got way behind in terms of our ability to understand the motivations of these people and to understand the impact it was having, particularly on young people.

"And then you fast-forward seven years, you've got a 14-year-old child in the Northwest of England being convicted of terrorism for trying to radicalize young people in Australia to carry out an attack in Melbourne on Mother's Day.

"All those factors were there in 2010; Choudhry was the first manifestation, and with serious consequences, in the developed world. We didn't open our eyes to the broader issues back then. We just dealt with it as a very serious attempted murder, and put it back in the box. We did not sit back, reflect, debrief, and consider the implications more broadly. It's something we should have done at that time, and it was most regrettable that we did not."

John's lessons are even more applicable in today's modern digital world. There is merit in studying the past and present incidents, considering the context of each, trying to gain a macro perspective and thinking about the bigger picture of what it could evolve into in the future.

When an event is looked at in isolation, it will always project a narrow view, which limits one's ability in preempting and preparing for the best defense response.

Likewise, in examining a cyberattack, it cannot be viewed in isolation. Effort and care should be taken in studying the source – is it just a random phishing attack, where is this coming from, are there other breaches instigated by an insider threat, is it a competitor that is trying to undermine your shareholder value, or did you happen to fall prey as a pawn in the grand scheme of geopolitical affairs?

When we look at the advancement and sophistication of these cyberattacks over recent years, we need to retain a holistic view of what these changing implications might mean for the overall organizational and individual risk.

Military leaders point out that capabilities take a long time to develop, but intentions can change overnight. In other words, the cyberattack impacts and response will not only center on current technology solutions, but also on what scenarios could happen in the future.

LEARNING FROM OUR PAST TO LEAD OUR FUTURE

While there are numerous management actions competing for attention, one clear priority that cuts across the public and private sectors is ensuring the leadership skills and capabilities of your team –especially the CISO or equivalent leadership role. To achieve any measure of success at dealing with cyber incidents, a CISO with the required background, accountability, training, real-life experiences, relationships, and tools to do the job is a must.

One such CISO is Mark Weatherford, currently the chief strategy officer at the National Cybersecurity Center and CISO at AlertEnterprise. Mark served previously as the deputy undersecretary for cybersecurity in the U.S. Department of Homeland Security (DHS) and vice president and CSO for the North American Electric Reliability Corporation (NERC), in addition to other senior leadership roles in cybersecurity.

While Mark was the CISO for the State of California in the mid-2000s, he experienced what organizations should *not* be doing when hiring for this vital role.

Because Mark was the first CISO in the state, it was important to him to put a face to the name of cabinet secretaries and agency heads. As such, he made the rounds to visit each of them and also to tell them about the governor's vision of Mark's statewide role and what he hoped to accomplish across state government. Mark also offered his assistance in everything from procurement to policy development to technology infrastructure to staffing. His proactive outreach seemed to be well-received and generally met with enthusiastic support.

At the same time, Mark also met the security leaders and their teams at all of the agencies. During the mid-2000s, almost none had a formally appointed CISO, but most had someone they could point to and call their security leader.

One exception was a large agency with significant citizen privacy responsibilities. Chief privacy officers were even more rare than CISOs at the time, so privacy issues were typically part of the CISO's portfolio of responsibilities. When Mark met with the leadership of this particular agency, he encouraged them to fill the CISO/security leader role as soon as possible since they were accepting a significant amount of risk by failing to have a single point of contact to guide the security and privacy efforts of the agency.

Mark recounts what happened next:

"A few months after the conversation with this agency head, I received a call from someone who said they had just taken the CISO role at this agency and would be very interested in meeting with me to understand how they could quickly integrate into the statewide security leadership group. I remember thinking how odd it was that, even though I had no real authority within this agency and they were under no formal obligation to ask my opinion, they had hired a CISO without consulting with me about writing the job description or even being part of the interview process. Red flag number one.

"When I met the new CISO for the first time I was impressed by their attitude and enthusiasm to pitch in and help me, as we were educating the legislature, crafting statewide security policies, and realigning statewide procurement of security products and services. Once again, however, I remember having a strange feeling that this person didn't seem to really have the kind of experience you would expect for someone taking over the security and privacy responsibilities of a fairly large organization. Red flag number two.

"We developed a pretty good rapport and began speaking once or twice a week when one day several months later I called this CISO but they were out of the office. I left a message to call me back. A week later I hadn't received a call back so I called again and left another message. Another week went by and no call back so I walked over to the agency and asked a receptionist about the CISO. My antennas immediately began wagging when the receptionist appeared nervous and I could tell they didn't want to talk to me. This was truly odd and . . . red flag number three.

"I walked back to my office and set up an appointment to meet with the agency head. As I walked into their office the following day, I could immediately tell something was askew. The agency head told me in an extremely embarrassed tone that the CISO was no longer employed there. Of course I was shocked and employed my best negotiation skill of sitting quietly, saying nothing, and waiting for them to talk. The rest of the story was slowly revealed.

"In their haste to hire a CISO, this agency had posted a job description, interviewed candidates, and hired a CISO – all without ever conducting a background investigation. Several months after hiring the CISO, a law enforcement organization met with the agency head and informed them that their new CISO had just been released from prison after serving a term for embezzlement. The CISO job was their first employment following a multiyear prison term. The agency head was personally mortified telling me this story and I can only imagine the look on my face as I heard the tale. They kept saying how embarrassed they were since I had offered to help them with hiring a CISO and they simply forgot in the urgency of filling the role.

"This is easily one of the most extreme examples I've been involved with where a simple background check could have eliminated a serious headache, but it is also one that taught me a good lesson. Not checking all the boxes during a critical process like hiring can be very painful."

No doubt, Mark's story highlights that building the right team to lead the overall cybersecurity program is a complex, difficult challenge. Beyond the CISO, most midsize and large organizations employ managers and/or directors to lead cybersecurity incident response and coordinate with the wider emergency management team throughout the enterprise

We cover much more about this in Chapter 4.

FREQUENT RANSOMWARE ATTACKS PROMPT RESPONSE CAPABILITY ENHANCEMENTS IN NEW YORK STATE

One thing that Dan learned from his high school football coach is that you can't keep doing the same things over and over and expect a different outcome or result. This concept has proven to be true within the cybersecurity community over the past decade, with the frequency and significant impact of ransomware attacks forcing changes to the strategies and tactics of incident response teams all across the globe. One set of ransomware stories, and how organizations adapted, comes from the former CISO for New York State government.

Deborah Snyder is a senior fellow at the Center for Digital Government, and she has a distinguished career in cybersecurity, most notably as the CISO for New York State until her retirement in late 2019. Deb has a wealth of helpful stories regarding cyber incident response with many practical implications. Specifically, she shared the following ransomware stories.

In the early hours of Sunday, April 9, 2017, Erie County Medical Center (ECMC), a 550-bed hospital in Buffalo, New York, was hit by a cyberattack. Staff noted a digital ransom note on a hospital workstation that demanded $44,000 in Bitcoin cryptocurrency for the key to unlock the hospital's files. Hackers had encrypted ECMC's data, impacting over 6,000 hospital computers.

When a ransomware attack hits a healthcare provider and brings down their computer systems, it can cause significant and life-threatening disruptions, interfering with patient care and public safety. The attack caused ECMC to shut down email and their website, and resulted in a six-week electronic health records systems outage. To avoid further damage, ECMC was forced to revert to paper records and process patient admissions, prescriptions, and other tasks manually for weeks. The FBI investigated, and a cybersecurity firm was brought in to support forensics and recovery efforts. The New York Office of Information Technology Services (ITS) and Cyber Incident

Response Team (CIRT) staff provided security guidance and support to the state department of health in protecting state systems and assets used by the facility. This incident was a wake-up call for many, as it dramatically highlighted the implications of interconnected systems and third-party access, and helped everyone involved grasp the serious potential for collateral impact. While ECMC didn't pay the ransom demand, the massive cyberattack came with a hefty price tag – nearly $10 million in hardware, software, response assistance, overtime, and other related expenses.

In another event, on August 30, 2017, the New York State Cyber Command Center (CYCOM) received a call indicating that Schuyler County had fallen victim to a sophisticated ransomware attack. The New York State CIRT team was immediately activated and an investigation confirmed that the attack involved SamSam – the same variant of ransomware ECMC had experienced. SamSam is typically distributed by compromising servers and using them to move laterally through the network to compromise additional devices. Given the touchpoints between state and county governments – both technical and programmatic – the government temporarily shut down network connectivity and access to the state's network and applications to prevent potential damage. Disruption to the county's 911 center and resulting risk to public safety was a major concern. This incident illustrated the potential for cyber events to have significant impact on public safety operations – fire, emergency medical, law enforcement, emergency communications, and other public safety partners – which in turn would directly and negatively impact the health and safety of the communities they serve. Fortunately, while some enhanced functions, such as integrated mapping, were impacted, the county was still able to receive and dispatch calls.

These incidents, along with the September 2017 Equifax breach that compromised personal data of 143 million Americans, including 8 million New Yorkers, served as a catalyst for formalizing comprehensive cyber disruption protocols. Coordinating resources, reporting, and response efforts across all involved state agencies – the

Office of Information Technology Services, Intelligence Center, and Division of Homeland and Emergency Security Services – enabled better defenses against cyber threats, protected citizens and government assets, and assured a coordinated, whole-of-state response to cyber incidents.

LIKE A BAD PENNY

From 2018 through 2019, ransomware attacks continued to accelerate in number and sophistication across the United States, targeting hospitals, state and local governments, and schools, causing major operational disruptions and financial impact. New York was not exempt.

On Saturday, March 30, 2019, the government cyber response team received a call from the City of Albany, which had experienced a major ransomware attack. Servers and workstations had been encrypted, resulting in significant operational impact across multiple systems and services. The attackers were demanding payment in Bitcoin to unlock systems. The City had engaged law enforcement, and FBI investigators were onsite. Within 30 minutes, the Cyber Command Center CIRT team members were onsite, helping City IT staff and the FBI with critical response actions and forensics.

City officials coordinated response and communications as the investigation and recovery efforts unfolded. The complex interdependencies between systems, data, critical functions, and services that incidents reveal never fail to amaze. Fully understanding these connections and program touchpoints in advance is critical, including linkages to county and state agencies' systems, potential collateral impact on program services, and related third-party dependencies.

New York's comprehensive whole-of-state cyber response protocol ensured coordinated state response efforts across state agencies. Emergency management alerted and assisted state agencies, such as the Department of Health, with connected systems and business processes and the impact on vital records. Routine executive briefings and the rapid exchange of information assured updates and sharing of available cyber threat intelligence with executives and participating agencies, including the New York State Intelligence Center, Division of Homeland and Emergency Security Services, and the Multi-State Information and Analysis Center (MS-ISAC).

While the attack temporarily disabled some city systems, backups of critical systems enabled recovery, and no ransom was paid. Reportedly, costs associated with remediation and recovery were roughly $300,000, for hardware, software, insurance, and other measures to increase the security and resiliency of the city's systems.[2]

In August 2019, the *New York Times* reported that more than 40 municipalities were victims of cyberattacks – from major cities such as Baltimore, Albany, and Laredo, Texas, to smaller towns including Lake City, Florida, one of the few cities to pay the ransom demand – about $460,000 in Bitcoin – because it determined that rebuilding its systems would be even more costly.[3]

EDUCATION SECTOR TARGETED BY CYBERCRIMINALS

It was Thursday, July 25, 2019, the day after Louisiana's governor declared a state of emergency following ransomware attacks on multiple public school districts in their state.[4] It was near the end of a particularly busy week, when the CYCOM hotline rang – never a good thing, as it generally meant that summer weekend plans would be replaced with handling an active incident.

New York's CIRT team responded to a call from the IT director of Lansing High School in Ithaca, reporting the presence of Ryuk ransomware on the school's IT infrastructure. The next call came from the school district in Watertown. They too had suffered a ransomware attack. A similar attack crippled the Syracuse city school district's computer system. Over the next days and weeks, calls were fielded from multiple school districts across New York State.

The Rockville Centre school district on Long Island was hit with Ryuk ransomware. They later paid almost $100,000 in ransom to restore their data; the school's insurance policy covered the payment. The same ransomware hit a neighboring school district in Mineola. They were able to restore data from backups taken offline over the summer and to rebuild the network.

The New York State Education Department notified all districts about the cyberattacks and coordinated the response to the incidents in affected educational agencies with the assistance of the State Office of Information Technology Services, CYCOM, and other state cyber-security teams, including the State Intelligence Center, Division of Homeland and Emergency Security Services, and the Multi-State Information and Analysis Center (MS-ISAC). Briefings with the New York State Department of Education and 11 Regional Information Centers (RICs) ensured that everyone had current information and focused support. The attacks were investigated, and the affected agencies recovered and implemented processes to mitigate recurrence.

All told, the New York State Department of Education reported that 16 school districts and one Board of Cooperative Educational Services (BOCES) had been compromised with ransomware.[5] As a precaution, the Education Department directed its regional information centers and big five school systems – Buffalo, Rochester, Syracuse, Yonkers, and New York City – to take the state's data warehouse offline to scan for malware and vulnerabilities.

The state's cohesive cyber disruption and incident response protocols worked well, enabling coordinated analysis and reporting and communications – essential in dealing with multiple and fast-moving attacks. A big win in this particular situation was a tool the CYCOM team developed to identify compromised domain controllers. Based on intelligence and high-confidence observations drawn from onsite and forensics analysis across multiple incidents, the team identified a consistent step in the multiphase attack taxonomy – how attacks unfold and work. Detection and intervention at this critical point in the sequence effectively disrupted the launch of damaging ransomware. The tool was shared with the Education Department, RICs, state universities, and other government entities to help proactively detect and defend against further attacks.

THE BATTLE CONTINUES

In 2021, adversaries upped their game with more sophisticated tactics and ambitious targets. As government organizations reeled from the impact of a global pandemic, the timing was ripe for another banner year for well-resourced cyber criminals and ransomware. One industry report, "The State of Ransomware in the US: Report and Statistics 2020," noted that 2,354 local governments, healthcare facilities, and schools were impacted by ransomware attacks in 2020.[6] For cyber criminals, government organizations pose an attractive target because they are often resource-constrained and maintain lots of valuable information such as Social Security numbers, birth and medical records, and financial account details. Faced with disruption of essential services to the public, government agencies are often faced with a tough decision – pay or try to restore their systems on their own.

On Christmas Day, 2020, the Albany (NY) International Airport was subject to a ransomware attack, and later paid a ransom to restore access to their data. The ransomware, attributed to a Russian threat actor, had spread to the airport's servers and backup servers from a managed service provider's systems. While the incident reportedly did not impact airport operations, TSA or airline computers, or expose sensitive data, it illustrated the need for organizations to exercise vigilance in protecting against such attacks and manage third-party/supply chain cyber risk exposure.

Some of the top takeaways from these New York State incidents include the importance of good cyber hygiene, due diligence, vigilance, and resilience. Keeping systems patched/current, secure design and configurations, access management – strong identity verification, authentication, and tightly managed privileged accounts, security awareness training to help users recognize phishing emails and other forms of social engineering, continuous monitoring and detection capabilities, solid backup and recovery platforms that assure rapid restoration of critical systems, and other protections can dramatically reduce the likelihood that ransomware will impact your organization's operations.

FIVE TAKEAWAYS

Shao Fei Huang, CISO of Singapore Land Transport Authority, highlighted his top three takeaways for business owners, board directors, and executives, and the stories from Mark Weatherford and Deb Snyder inspired the last two.

The World Will Never Be Immune to Cyberattacks

Organizations and businesses need to ensure that their cybersecurity strategies are centered on people, process, and technology. Traditionally, the focus has been on IT, and even CISO appointments have been given to the IT staff, reporting to the CIO. Aside from this reporting line, which would result in a conflict of interest, it is key for CISOs to carry a large responsibility in the organization and to be given the authority to raise the alarm if something is not right, even if this relates to the actions of their executives or their decisions.

In appointing CISOs, CEOs and boards should ensure that the individual is equipped with qualities such as strong technical expertise in cybersecurity, business acumen, crisis management skills, and a soft skill that has been often neglected: a flair for public speaking, especially to senior executives and stakeholders.

No businesses want to be a sitting duck, which is why it is critical for the CISO leadership to be appropriately identified and strategically placed in the organization. The CISO and team play a huge role in steering and executing the cybersecurity program, ensuring that appointed parties are responsible and accountable. The cybersecurity function (ideally led by a CISO) has to be deliberated at the C-suite and reported at the board level.

Cybersecurity Is a Business Risk Issue

More and more people are coming to the realization that cybersecurity is not just an IT issue. The onslaught of recent cybersecurity supply chain attacks and identity breaches on a global scale is a clear sign that it is not a matter of if, but when, an organization discovers it has undergone a cybersecurity attack, whether directly or indirectly. Boards and executives need to understand the "system" at play in how these attacks and the damaging downstream consequences pan out. They do not just center around the IT departments of their organizations, but impact every member within the organization and externally, including each of their customers.

How the organization reacts, responds, and learns from cyber incidents is very much a reflection of the organization's values and capability.

The Double-Edged Sword of Zero Trust

CEOs and boards need to understand what zero trust is and how blindly adopting zero trust could stand in the way of effective incident response (IR) when cyber emergencies happen. The zero trust approach, by definition, is to "never trust, always verify."

The concept is not about making a system or network trustworthy. It is about eliminating trust from the decision loop. While useful as a broad cybersecurity concept, boards and executives need to carefully apprise the risks that come with such an approach, especially if their cyber response playbooks require the use of a service, software update, or patch that cannot be verified quickly enough to contain the incident. Often it may be useful to identify trade-offs early on in a risk-based approach and take an approach of pre-verifying "verified" systems, vendors, or partners for situations like this.

Pick the Right Person to Lead the Effort

Mark Weatherford's story highlights the vital need to do your homework when selecting a CISO or other top cybersecurity leaders. Much more on this in Chapters 2 and 4, but it must be emphasized upfront that you need someone accountable for the cybersecurity program with the knowledge, experience, a good understanding of organizational culture, and the authority to get things done.

Beyond background checks and impressive resumes (or CVs), does your CSO, CISO, or other top cybersecurity executive excel at relationships in a 360-degree manner with staff, peers, executive management, clients, and vendor relationships? You can strengthen the leader's effectiveness by surrounding him or her with the right mix of professionals who close gaps in weak areas. Finally, does the CISO's vision of success align with the executive board?

Act and Adjust with Resilience as the Cyber Situation Evolves

The eye-opening stories from Deb Snyder reveal an ability to adapt and remain resilient as cyberattacks grow and become more impactful.

In the next few chapters, we will demonstrate how an effective cybersecurity program with relevant strategies, tactics, plans, and playbooks grew to become best practices and eventually standard practices for cyber defense teams worldwide. Leaders can't wait for a perfect solution and allow indecision in the midst of cyberbattles. Rather, they must act and adapt based on threat intelligence, robust information sharing, and a clear understanding of priorities with the tools available to fully utilize their team's skill sets.

Fail to Plan or Plan to Fail: Cyber Disruption Response Plans and Cyber Insurance

Intellectuals solve problems, geniuses prevent them.

—Albert Einstein

Could it be time to start over with a blank sheet of paper? When was the last time your organization performed a comprehensive, top-to-bottom examination of its cybersecurity program? This assessment includes cyber protections, framework(s), processes used, tools used, standards used, threat intelligence capabilities, cyber incident response capabilities, budget, legal aspects, emergency management procedures, contracts, network architecture, protections in place, cyber insurance, cyber playbooks, penetration tests, internal and external partnerships, staffing (skillsets and vacancy levels), training, and more.

Perhaps a data breach (or other security incident) prompted this review, or auditors have highlighted significant material weaknesses. In some cases, a new executive leader demands changes, upgrades, or a new way of thinking.

The reality is that, regardless of the reason(s), every organization needs to consider such a cyber review on a regular basis. The dramatic changes faced by all organizations, including new technology paradigms, evolving cyberthreats, increasing customer expectations for digital transformation, and radical shifts caused by major events like the COVID-19 pandemic, demand a fresh look at cybersecurity at least as often as you upgrade critical technology infrastructure.

But how do we do this? What about your legacy environment? Consider the following case study.

THE MAKING OF THE MICHIGAN CYBER INITIATIVE

It was time to reinvent the cybersecurity program – again.

What was about to be implemented would become best practices (and later versions would become standard practices) for numerous state and local government cybersecurity programs, incident response plans, government playbooks, public–private partnerships, cyber disruption response strategies, statewide tabletop exercises, and much more in governments around the globe.

In fact, the Michigan Cyber Range,[1] the Michigan Cyber Disruption Response Strategy of 2013,[2] the more detailed Michigan Cyber Disruption Response Plan of 2015,[3] the Michigan Cyber Civilian Corps,[4] the North American International Cyber Summit series,[5] and other cybersecurity programs launched as part of the Michigan Cyber Initiative have been studied,[6] emulated, repeated, built upon, and become a leading model for numerous government efforts and standard approaches to cybersecurity governance.[7]

Michigan had previously won awards, received global recognition, and established the national standard for state and local governments to emulate for information security management in the mid-2000s. Its teams partnered extensively with the best and the brightest in the private sector and the U.S. Department of Homeland Security (DHS) on cyber solutions.

But life moved on, and so did many of the experts and leadership team members.

After serving as Michigan's first CISO from May 2002 until January 2009, Dan moved on to become Michigan's chief technology officer over all technology infrastructure, including data centers, help desks, network management, desktop and mobile support, cloud services, system administration, and much more. This enterprise-wide deputy director of infrastructure role supported the state's 10 million citizens and over 50,000 state employees and contractors. The CTO managed over 750 state employees as well as several hundred contract staff, with an annual budget of more than $200 million.

But when Rick Snyder, the former CEO of Gateway Computers, became Michigan's governor in January 2011, a new opportunity arose. Dan turned down several private sector job offers and a chance to become the U.S. Department of Defense (DoD) CISO in order to lead Michigan's development of a comprehensive new security program overseeing physical and cybersecurity in government. He wore many hats in this new role, including managing statewide cyber coordination efforts that cut across public and private sectors.

Governor Snyder's cyber vision included vastly improving overall state toolsets and capabilities, educating the masses, university research, economic development with tech companies, new involvement with the National Guard, a new state police emergency coordination and fusion center that incorporated cyber, P-20 cyber programs, federal law enforcement involvement in programs, new grants, and much more. Michigan would also lead these cybersecurity efforts within the National Governors Association (NGA), and the governor was recognized as cutting-edge regarding cybersecurity advancements globally.

While still formally functioning as Michigan CTO in the spring and summer of 2011, Dan spent the vast majority of his time (including nights and weekends) working on this "secret" security project with intense urgency. With the full support of the governor and Michigan CIO David Behen, he brought together a diverse group of technology, security, and business experts across multiple sectors in Michigan to create and lead what became known as the Michigan Cyber Initiative.[8]

The in-person meetings started with a series of workshops and vision sessions with top experts from academia, government, leading companies, and more. These sessions would later continue in what were called "Kitchen Cabinet"[9] meetings, with CIOs (and later as a separate meeting with public/private CISOs) from across the state meeting monthly on action items.

While many of the elements of the Michigan Cyber Initiative fall beyond the scope of this book, it is essential to understand that a robust incident response capability was a core deliverable. Here is a brief excerpt from that initial document's executive summary:

Elements of Michigan's Cyber Threat Response – . . . *cyberattacks pose a real and serious hazard to our safety and security. Both situations can result in long-term implications that are costly and often produce irreversible damage. Therefore, Michigan is approaching cybersecurity with the same level of commitment when preparing for and responding to threats to the natural environment:*

Prevention – taking steps to keep an event from happening

Early Detection and Rapid Response – discovering an attack in its early stages and responding to minimize the consequences

Control, Management, and Restoration – taking appropriate steps to minimize and contain the effects of an event and return to normal operations

Through continued research, education, and collaboration in these areas, the state of Michigan will positively leverage its people, businesses, and technology expertise to deter and prevent attacks against our digital infrastructure. With proper execution, each of these elements will secure our cyber ecosystem, enhance

Michigan's leadership in this critical 21st-century arena and provide new economic development opportunities in our state. . . .

Beyond the creation of the initial strategy, many other steps were essential to the immense success of the Michigan Cyber Initiative. One element was the very public backing of top leadership – in this case, the governor, who led the 2011 Michigan Cyber Summit.[10] This summit was the biggest event of its kind to that point; Michigan's congressional delegation, federal government leaders, and top private sector tech companies (such as Facebook, Microsoft, Google, Symantec, AT&T, Comcast, Unisys, and IBM) were speakers.

Why was that initial cyber summit so important? Because the executive leadership in state government and in the private sector, as well as federal partners, knew (and heard firsthand) that the cyber strategy was a top priority that required their attention and actions, and they agreed to be held accountable for their specific deliverables that were planned with dates assigned.

That event set the stage for what was to come. DHS Secretary Janet Napolitano provided the keynote; the importance of cyber issues had finally grown to the point that this was the first time that a DHS secretary discussed cybersecurity outside the Capitol Beltway.[11]

Governor Snyder quickly raised the bar: "If people walk away tomorrow saying that we had a nice conference with good speakers, we will have failed. We need everyone walking away saying that it is time to act now on cyber – whatever their role."[12]

CONFRONTING CYBER EMERGENCIES: THE MICHIGAN CYBER DISRUPTION RESPONSE PLAN

The CSO "Kitchen Cabinet" was a group of leading government and private sector CISOs from around the state of Michigan who met monthly to share cyber best practices, strategies, and tactical plans. Beyond peer networking, the top cybersecurity leaders from their organizations voted on the priorities for statewide issues that needed to be addressed for the benefit of all.

The group worked together to establish structured documents on a variety of topics, including information sharing regarding cyberthreats, action plans, and joint attention to critical gaps in capability. Note that the individual organizations developed and confidentially shared their internal cyber incident response policies, standards, and plans for day-to-day escalation of cyber incidents. The need was identified to address a cyber emergency with statewide impact, assuming that Governor Snyder declared a formal emergency via an executive order or directive.

In partnership with the private sector companies that owned and operated Michigan's critical infrastructure, the first Michigan Cyber Disruption Response Strategy mapped out a clear communication strategy and the necessary actions following a major cyber incident in the state.[13] This document was studied by FEMA and other states, and a later version became a best practice for all 50 states.[14]

In 2016, the National Association of State CIOs (NASCIO) published a Cyber Disruption Response Planning Guide[15] that offered:

- A call to action for states to develop state cyber disruption response plans that include: a governance structure that clearly designates who is in charge in a given event or phase of an event; development of a risk profile for state assets; collaboration among the various agencies that have cyber responsibility; and a communication plan to ensure that the right people have the right information as early as possible so they can respond effectively.
- A checklist for states to work with in developing progress toward a cyber disruption response operating discipline.
- A cross-functional process description that can be used as a starting point for states to develop their own unique cross-functional process for orchestrated planning and response at various threat levels.

Some of the key questions and decision points in the checklist include:

- *Establish decision points mapped to the lifecycle of an event, including determining threat level, action plans, and resource allocation.*
- *How do we classify an event and its severity?*
- *What are the critical decision points for each classification?*
- *How are decision points staged, coordinated, and/or integrated*
- *How is information shared, tracked, and managed?*
- *Who is responsible for escalating or de-escalating a cyber event?*
- *Who has lead responsibility at each point?*
- *Who has supportive responsibility at each point?*
- *Who is responsible for after action, evaluation, reports, and improvements?*
- *Who is involved in cyber disruption planning, and have they been consulted and included?*

Outline the responsible party(ies) from, and any decision rights for, the following entities:

Office of the Governor

State CIOs office and CISO

Homeland Security

Emergency Management Agencies

Public Safety, incl. State Police

Fusion Centers

National Guard

Other State Agencies/Health, Transportation, Education, Regional Partners (other states, tribes, nations, and territories)

Utilities, Private Sector, Industry and Service Providers (e.g., Health)

Intergovernmental Agencies (federal and local)

Other _____

These state cyber emergency response documents evolved over time. In mid-2019, the National Governors Association published an issue briefing covering State Cyber Disruption Response Plans.[16] Topics covered included:

- State Cybersecurity and Response Planning
- State Cyber Disruption Response Plans
- The National Cyber Incident Response Plan
- Recommendations for Creating a State Cyber Disruption Response Plan
  - State Cyber Response Plans and the Emergency Operations Plan
  - Threat Schemas and Plan Activation
  - Lead and Supporting Agencies
  - Roles and Responsibilities
  - Cyber UCG and Cybersecurity Response Teams
- Appendix (With Table Showing Public Plans in States and Where the State Plan Resides)

U.S. FEDERAL GOVERNMENT GUIDANCE ON SECURITY INCIDENT HANDLING

At the federal level, the National Institute of Standards and Technology (NIST) has released several important standards and documents. To start, NIST Special Publication 800-61 Revision 2 – Computer Security Incident Handling Guide was last released in 2012.[17] The Guide starts with this abstract:

> *Computer security incident response has become an important component of information technology (IT) programs. Because performing incident response effectively is a complex undertaking, establishing a successful incident response capability requires*

substantial planning and resources. This publication assists organizations in establishing computer security incident response capabilities and handling incidents efficiently and effectively. This publication provides guidelines for incident handling, particularly for analyzing incident-related data and determining the appropriate response to each incident. The guidelines can be followed independently of particular hardware platforms, operating systems, protocols, or applications.

An organization's cybersecurity incident management process is a part of the organization's business, technology, and cyber program that includes other components included in the Michigan Cyber Initiative, such as training, threat intelligence, and the Michigan Cyber Disruption Response Plan. An organization's strategic and tactical plans must address many types of business risk, and cyber risk is just one aspect to consider.

The internationally recognized guidance contained in the Cybersecurity Framework,[18] or CSF, offers five core components (Figure 2.1): identify, protect, detect, respond, and recover (other frameworks use other labels). Note: The NIST CSF is a subset of NIST 800-53 and also shares controls found in ISO 27002. The NIST CSF takes parts of ISO 27002 and parts of NIST 800-53, but is not inclusive of both.

FIGURE 2.1   Five Core Functions of NIST Cybersecurity Framework
Source: "The Five Functions," NIST, https://www.nist.gov/cyberframework/online-learning/five-functions.

There are differences in opinion about whether NIST or SANS offers the best incident response framework. A helpful article from ATT offers a comparison guide between the two approaches.[19]

While there are many different names used to describe an organization's internal incident response plan, every plan must establish the incident response policies and procedures to ensure that an organization can effectively address computer security incidents that may have compromised sensitive and/or personally identifiable information (PII), or have a serious impact on an organization's ability to accomplish its missions.

An incident response plan also specifies the organizational methods for preparation, detection, analysis, eradication, and containment of an incident. The plan describes, in detail, the actions that an incident response team will take upon notification of an incident that could represent, but is not limited to, unauthorized access, alteration or compromise, denial of service (DoS), malicious code, or misuse.

The following laws and regulations are applicable to incident planning:

- State-specific data breach reporting laws as listed by the National Conference of State Legislatures (NCSL)[20]
- Federal Information Security Management Act (FISMA) of 2002 [Title III, PL 107-347]
- Management of Federal Information Resources [OMB Circular A-130]
- Records Management by Federal Agencies [44 USC 31]
- Safeguarding Against and Responding to the Breach of Personally Identifiable Information [OMB Memo M-07-16]

The Resources section at the end of the book offers additional standards and guidance that are useful for understanding incident planning, in addition to NIST Special Publication 800-61 Revision 2, mentioned earlier.

Many organizations cover incident response under the wider umbrella of emergency management planning, and take what is known as an "all hazards" approach to emergency response. For example, regardless of what caused an incident like a power outage or the contamination of a water supply, the response processes would be similar. Of course, the root cause analysis would be different for a cyberattack and a thunderstorm.

POSITIVE SECURITY AND RISK MANAGEMENT FOR INTERNATIONAL ORGANIZATIONS

First released in 2005, ISO/IEC 27001 is an internationally recognized standard that sets out the specification for an information security management system (ISMS). ISO/IEC 27001:2013 is the most current version of the standard and incorporates changes made in 2017. The standard contains a set of best practices to enable organizations to implement an effective risk management system and strategize their security investments.

An increasing number of private and public sector organizations in Australia and the Association of Southeast Asian Nations (ASEAN) now insist that their suppliers and contractors demonstrate effective management of information security in compliance with ISO/IEC 27001. Privasec (*a Sekuro company*) has observed that positive security and risk management outcomes are a driver for companies determined to demonstrate their commitment to security.

Romain Rallu, CEO of cybersecurity consulting firm Privasec, explains, "By establishing a security roadmap with ownership amongst the founders and senior leadership for a company-wide focus on security, implementing security as a culture and baking it into operations has helped many businesses scale and increase enterprise market credibility."

As one of the fastest-growing independent governance, risk, and compliance security consulting firms in the region, Privasec has partnered with large and medium-size organizations across industries. Out of the many success stories, Romain shared a key case study of a multinational company that Privasec brought through the ISMS journey:

"With close to 10,000 staff located in more than 200 offices, the company was made of diverse lines of businesses across 20 countries, some organic and some through acquisition. We had to engage stakeholders worldwide. This required us to build a comprehensive plan, leverage the unique diversity of our team to engage using different languages in nearly all time zones. We also had to build a program of work which allowed flexibility to cater for constant operations changes, inherent to a company of this size with a global footprint. Finally, we had to work closely with the certification body and their audit team to plan, facilitate and guide audits in all regions."

Despite the seemingly large magnitude of the task, Romain commented on the impact of this far-reaching program: "This gave our client a unique opportunity to capitalize on the momentum to grow a network of security champions which enabled them to identify and respond to security events faster and in a more coordinated manner. This ensures continuity of operations and unified communications, which is paramount.

"With the continuous news of security incidents, people judge organizations more on their response to an incident than on having the incident," he elaborates. "Your market, as well as many regulators, can forgive an incident but won't forgive a poor or disjointed response."

This multinational company was positioned as an early adopter of security in their industry, which gave, and continues to give, them an edge when pitching for work. It also raised the awareness of domestic executives and allowed the company to start "baking in" security in their culture, the same way quality and occupational health and safety were, thus not only improving their response to incidents but their resilience as well.

Ang Leong Boon, Head of IT Security at the National University of Singapore (NUS), known for their academic programs ranked among the top globally, sat down with Shamane in her *Mega C-Suite Stories* podcast recording and walked through key milestones of their security journey.

"Let me go back in time, to more than 10 years back when cybersecurity wasn't a thing globally. Back then, it was more of reacting to various incidents that might occur in an organization. For example, you might have a malware infection that could lead to a worm spreading through your network, which would require immediate response. That was when NUS formed our Computer Emergency Response Team (CERT); we were one of Singapore's first CERTs.[21] As the name suggests, the main task was to perform incident response. In a university especially, there are many incidents where we would need to handle, whether it's internally, perhaps from mischievous students, or external hackers trying to breach our network.

"With that as the foundation, it created a technically strong team as I believe that the best way to learn about cybersecurity is through experiencing and handling real world attacks. The main reason the team has remained very competent is because of our contact with various kinds of incidents that we've handled. Quite a number of our team members right now, including myself, started out doing incident response, and now branched out to other areas of work, which includes looking at detection and prevention in a timely manner."

Leong Boon revealed that a major cyber incident years ago triggered a positive change in the way the university has executed their cybersecurity strategy since then. "We were one of the first to do our own phishing drills, as early as 2013, before these phishing drill platforms became popular. We have always been investing a lot in security awareness training, but I would say that the incident actually created a culture change across our entire organization."

In 2017, NUS, along with other local universities, suffered from one of the largest security breaches in Singapore as a result of a bid to steal government and research data. "Of course, this was overshadowed by the 2018 SingHealth data breach, but it was the biggest-ever attack the

University suffered from. This was the work of a sophisticated nation-state threat actor." Leong Boon continued, "Through that one incident, everyone realized what it was like to fight a real battle out there. It was the first time we had a full-blown war room. We lived and ate in that room for two weeks or more. It was also the first time our different colleagues in IT sat with us together in that room, to investigate, find root causes, to resolve issues. Through that, it was an experience all of them remembered, and one that probably no one wants to relive."

CHANGES IN THE PLANNING APPROACH POST-INCIDENT

Leong Boon explained the security growth of the university since the incident: "Since then, we've put in many more controls because we've experienced firsthand what it was like to be attacked and breached by an attacker of such sophistication. Much effort was dedicated into acquiring capabilities for us to detect threats in a timely fashion. Comparing and contrasting to previously where we were doing mostly incident response, which is more of a reaction (because we are reacting to an incident only after it has happened, or only after they have been reported), we are now moving to a more proactive or even predictive approach, where we use various technologies to help us detect these threats before they escalate.

"Part of what we are focusing on right now is to leverage cyber threat intelligence to provide us with an added layer of visibility of who might be attacking us, and different kinds of tactics, techniques and procedures (TTPs) they could be using."

He also commented on the difference it makes when there is a connection between the different functions and security within the organization, "Many times, we see that there is a disconnect between different IT functions when it comes to cybersecurity. For example, for our infrastructure colleagues, they would be most concerned with availability. . . . However, through the incident, where we were all in the same war room together, we have realized that our colleagues now also view security as a very important aspect, and they have started to see security through our lens."

On the changes in the other IT function approaches, Leong Boon added, "They have started to integrate security as part of their project implementation, starting right from the planning and foundation stage. This is something that I feel would only have been possible if you were part of that experience of being in that war room, and you would not want to relive that. And how would you not want to relive that? That is to get all of your systems secured right from the start, and even then, as an ongoing process, you would want to keep your systems constantly patched."

The key is that security is no longer an afterthought, but something the team actively considers right from the get-go, as they know the situation they want to avoid. "The incident ended up being a very powerful lesson that created a lot of positivity in the organization."

The Cyber Security Agency of Singapore (CSA) offers a helpful incident response checklist structured around the IPDRR (Identify, Protect, Detect, Response, Recover) framework as part of their GOsafeonline awareness campaign.[22] Once response plans are written, the important tasks of training staff and testing the plan via tabletop exercises must be addressed. These topics are covered further in Chapter 3.

THE WISCONSIN GOVERNMENT APPROACH TO CYBERSECURITY INCIDENT RESPONSE

To offer a different perspective on this important topic of planning for, and responding to, cyber incidents, we turned to Bill Nash, a respected government CISO who was involved in numerous security incidents. Bill was the CISO for the State of Wisconsin from June 2013 until February 2021.

At the state government level, Wisconsin has centralized IT infrastructure operations while agencies manage endpoints and applications. In addition, Wisconsin is a Home Rule State, which from the cyber perspective means that IT is managed locally, and local law enforcement has jurisdiction for the community's cybercrimes.

Within the Wisconsin public sector, there are more than 60 state agencies, commissions, and attached boards; 72 counties; 1,950 municipalities; 11 American Indian nations and tribal communities; 444 school districts; 16 public technical colleges; 31 public colleges and universities; 81 municipal electric utilities; 575 drinking water utilities; 1 gas utility, and 600 wastewater utilities that all need to be aware and prepared for a cyberattack.

Keeping the public sector in Wisconsin secure was going to require collaboration with all levels of government. Shortly after Bill was hired as the State's CISO, the Wisconsin leadership team took a trip over the lake to meet with the Michigan technology and security teams to discuss the Michigan Cyber Civilian Corp.

Bill elaborated on setting up their program: "We also shared our plans for Wisconsin to get the Michigan team's input. This led to the Wisconsin Cyber Responses Teams (CRTs) that were started in 2015 with $50,000 of Homeland Security Grant funding with the goal to recruit and train local government IT staff to respond to cyber incidents. The concept was based on the Federal Emergency Management Agency's (FEMA) draft pre-decisional "National Incident Management System (NIMS) Resource Management for Cybersecurity" model, and the goal was to have 3 teams of 10 volunteer cybersecurity personnel aligned to Wisconsin Emergency Management regions.

"The grant funding continued to grow each year and still provides reimbursement for the training classes, covers lodging for exercises, and provides incident response equipment for Cyber-Response Team (CRT) members. The CRT member's employer is responsible for covering their CRT member's salary, benefits, and other expenses while participating in CRT activities. CRT participation benefits the member's organization by providing training and experience to their employee that helps to better secure their organization.

"The CRT program is a whole community approach to provide training, experience, share intelligence, and provide cyber assistance (like mutual aid) to Wisconsin's public sector organizations in a cyber incident. In addition to individual and group cyber training classes, the CRT members participate in one to two exercises per year that include the Wisconsin National Guard cyber team, the Wisconsin Statewide Intelligence Center/Fusion Center cyber analysts and private sector CIKR members. These exercises validate cyber response plans and procedures for the deployment of WI cyber resources in response to a cyber incident.

"There are currently 78 CRT members, representing counties, cities, towns, villages, tribal communities, K–12 schools, and technical colleges. Even though the CRT capability is still being developed, CRT team members have already responded to over 35 Wisconsin local government cyber incidents either onsite with a team or provided guidance via phone since inception. In addition to the CRT responding to incidents, they also analyze threats, and exchange critical cybersecurity information with trusted state and federal partners. On the prevention side, the CRT has assisted local units of government with vulnerability assessments, best practice recommendations, and cyber security awareness activities.

"We also offer full-scale, inter-team, cyber-response exercises training for these key organizations.

"The teams are not intended to compete with private sector resources but are there to support local government organizations in Wisconsin in mitigating, responding to, and recovering from a significant cyber incident, in which private sector resources are not available."

A PRIVATE SECTOR PERSPECTIVE ON COMPUTER SECURITY INCIDENT RESPONSE

Mike Davis is the current CISO at ExactlyIT Inc., a digital transformation company. He began his career in the U.S. military, served as

Director of IT Security (functioning CISO) for the American Bureau of Shipping (ABS) and was the CISO for alliantgroup.

Here are Mike's top recommendations and his overall perspectives on building a cyber incident response program:

"There is never any substitute for being well prepared ahead of time. We must have an actionable Computer Security Incident Response (CSIR) Plan in place and well-practiced.

"I always start with NIST (and this is an overall reference):

- NIST SP 800-61r2 (as mentioned in our earlier government section), followed by
- CREST Cyber Security Incident Response Guide;[23] and
- Cynet Incident Response Plan Templates (six to choose from/templates too)[24]

"For cyber security incidents and emergencies, the essence of the CSIR plan should be twofold:

1. Rapid identification and containment of the incident; those immediate actions that are critical to have harmonized between OPS/IT, Security and your SOC/MDR, and
2. Sample messaging for initial notification of a service disruption and follow-on details of the incident for the media group.

"The rest of the CSIR plan should have supporting details on other processes (forensics, restoration, etc.), whereas they are not as time critical as stopping the attack. The immediate actions need to be practiced frequently – recommend every clearly unusual computer event be treated as a potential incident as a practice session, at least between OPS/IT and security. This also exercises the communications and coordination processes between them and the SOC/MDR team. It's all too easy for too many players to pile on and offer suggestions (especially managers), while the immediate actions get delayed.

"Playbooks are essential, as no one has the CSIR plan ready at all times, and even then, there is a lot of added material for the steps after containment that can be followed using the actual plan. Immediate actions for all parts of the team need to be created (again, especially OPS, SEC, SOC/MDR with something shorter for management to follow, and also the messaging group: media, legal, CISO, etc.). Playbooks need to be always accessible, and so digitally stored where all the players can access them, including the service desk.

"Recommend a digital war room be established, with rooms for the action team, management, and the media group, where the CSIR on-scene leader keeps the three aligned. Always best to have the event status messages in one spot as well . . . with various versions for employees, clients, and external. Then all messages are sent using various mediums using a link to those messages, which can be updated and also have stricter access control. In addition, it's harder to send the information to others (like social media) and so that the messages are structured and continue.

"Always have a non-email communications process as well, since compromise[d] accounts can monitor the email traffic and know your status, next moves.

"In the communications section of the CSIR plan, address all the potential contacts and when they are notified and by whom. This includes law enforcement, outside counsel, and your cyber insurance agent, to name a few. Address if/when you would consider paying the ransom, and even then, do that only through your cyber insurance agent. In the CSIR comms section, make it clear that only legal ever calls a data event/incident a "breach" – as the reporting clock starts then, and attorney/client privilege is invoked and communications can then be considered as exculpatory evidence. . . ."

INCIDENT RESPONSE AND CYBER INSURANCE

More and more public and private sector organizations are purchasing cyber insurance that covers them should a costly incident occur.

While there are many great resources that describe the pros and cons of purchasing cyber insurance,[25] it must be stressed that having cyber insurance *does not* relieve an organization from responsibilities of due diligence in protecting sensitive information. These duties include a robust incident response program and repeatable processes being implemented by well-trained incident response teams.

On the contrary, cyber insurance policies require comprehensive security programs with lengthy checklists to ensure that adequate protections are in place and followed, before cyber insurance policies are even executed. The National Governors Association published a two-page public sector guide to cyber insurance in 2019,[26] and the practice of using cyber insurance has grown rapidly since. However, after large losses from insurers in 2020, cyber liability insurance premiums are rising fast as well.

According to a range of hospital CISOs we spoke with in mid-2021 who worked with cyber insurance companies, current trends include:

- 2021 renewal rates are typically 35–50% over those in 2020.
- Ransomware riders are often required.
- Ransomware questionnaires are more complex.
- Scanning the network environments is often performed before policies are issued.
- There is often a proactive assessment of enterprise risk before policies are executed.

To examine cyber insurance in more detail and offer recommendations to consider, we turned to Mark Stamford, the founder and CEO of OccamSec, a cyber security company based in New York City. OccamSec works with organizations across the world to identify how they could be attacked and how to prevent attacks, such as hacking networks, applications, vehicles, and anything else with a computer in it; hackers also break into buildings, wear disguises, and conduct intelligence work.

According to Mark, these are the first things you need to know if you're thinking of making the investment in cyber insurance:

- Ask yourself, what controls are the insurers requiring you to have in place to issue a policy? Some of these may not necessarily apply to your company, so what happens then? There tend to be blanket requirements, but depending on what you do and how you do it this may not be practical.
- Thoroughly read all war clause fine print, especially given how difficult attribution is for an attack. "War clauses" have caused problems in the past – cyberattacks believed to have originated with a nation-state (such as Wannacry) enable insurers to not pay out on policies (since a cyberattack is considered an act of war).
- Find out if there will be any additional costs.
- Brokers are really more useful in finding you the best deal than if you try to shop around yourself.

Going deeper into specific tips, here are recommended questions at each stage of an incident.

Before an incident:

1. Review your policy: What do you need to have in place, or need to be doing, to meet the requirements of your policy? Do you need to perform regular security assessments? Incident response exercises? What tools is the insurer requiring you to have? Keep in mind that cyber insurers are flying in the dark as much as it seems everyone else is.
2. War clauses: Are they in there? If so, who gets to decide what's an "act of war"?
3. What will your policy cover? Notifications to customers? Lost revenue? Other?
4. What happens if the incident is caused by a third party? How will that be covered?

5. Does the insurer provide support during an incident? What's the service level agreement on that? (It's not always very quick.) What's the coverage if there are approved incident response (IR) vendors?

6. Do you have an IR process? Have you tested it?

During an incident:

1. Check with the insurer about whether they will provide support, and if you need to notify them, or otherwise deal with the incident.

2. Make sure you document your incident handling (this should be covered in your IR policy).

After an incident:

1. Keep evidence to show what you did before and during the incident. They are going to ask you for that.

2. Be aware that insurers are looking for "gotchas" to not pay. There are several recent examples where insurers did pay, and companies had to pay the money back due to a lack of due diligence in areas such as patching vulnerabilities.

Mark concludes, "I would also consider what you need the insurance to cover, and why. How much is the policy going to pay out? And is that going to cover your possible costs? Is it worth the investment?

"Organizations that experience a successful cyber attack will find themselves required to undertake a range of responsive actions with some degree of urgency, often at significant cost. This is not just related to technology and/or cyber consulting, but legal fees, media management, and customer support, and even compensation can add up very quickly."

Michael Cracroft is the former chief security and technology officer of Service NSW, a New South Wales Government executive agency in Australia that provides one-stop access to government services. Originally from the UK, Michael has been leading digital transformation initiatives in Australia, including public cloud migrations and modernizing technology services for community platforms to leverage cloud-native architectures. Some of his other achievements include cyber risk management for the highly successful Digital Driver Licence program and the award-winning Covid-Safe Check-in app, which saw mobile app usage increase from 600,000 to a staggering 6 million customers during 2021.

Having signed up for cyber insurance coverage for Service NSW a few years ago, Michael shared his thoughts on the matter:

"Cyber insurance is a complementary measure that should be considered part of any defense in-depth design in addition to, not in place of, actionable controls. Your board will be glad that you secured cyber insurance beforehand, if an attack should occur and the worst-case scenario happens.

When you look at the economics, it will be interesting to see what the cyber insurers are going to do to manage the increasing volumes of organizations needing to submit a claim from a cyber attack. When you consider this, it seems likely that a couple of things may happen:

1. Cyber premiums will start to rise and smaller organizations may start to get priced out of the cyber insurance market.

   The implications may be a loss of ability to appropriately manage breaches. Consequently, we may see organizations struggling more with the ethics of incident response, such as paying ransomware or failing to notify impacted customers.
2. Insurers may start to require organizations to validate their security compliance posture as part of balancing their premiums. This may translate to a broader community-wide adoption of cyber compliance standards, such as ISO 27001 or SOC2, which may have the benefit of raising the bar of industry cyber maturity.

"We have recently seen new partnerships forming between public cloud providers and insurance companies, which allude to cyber insurance being packaged with the services – if you appropriately configure and secure your cloud. If this becomes a de-facto relationship, we may see those organizations running on-premises infrastructure disadvantaged in securing insurance and needing to apply increasingly complex assurances to secure a reasonable premium.

"It is essential to address cyber resilience measures before an attack occurs, as it seems clear the cost of being compromised is climbing and boards need to understand that cyber insurance is not a control which absolves them of responsibility. However, it is important that we acknowledge any system may potentially be breached and in those circumstances, cyber insurance is a risk mitigation that should not be underestimated."

CHAPTER 3

Practice Makes Perfect: Exercises, Cyber Ranges, and BCPs

We are what we do. Excellence, then, is not an act, but a habit.

—Aristotle

An April 2021 headline in the *Wall Street Journal* read: "NATO Wargame Examines Cyber Risk to Financial System," followed with, "Financial industry helped plan scenarios in which widespread disruption would hit banks and other firms."[1]

The North Atlantic Treaty Organization (NATO), with more than 2,000 participants from 30 countries, ran its annual Locked Shields wargame exercise on April 13–16, 2021. For the first time ever, the scenario explored how widespread attacks on a fictional nation's infrastructure might strike at activities critical to keeping the global financial system functioning.

From Mastercard to NatWest Group PLC to the Swiss Computer Emergency Readiness Team, numerous experts planned scenarios to help test emergency response plans and examine how ready financial teams were for unplanned disruptions.

But this four-day event was more than just a tabletop exercise, where executives typically sit around a table and discuss how they will handle various emergency situations. NATO called this simulation a "live-fire" exercise, which involved actual attacks against systems set up with cyber teams defending against the attacks.

Although this exercise was the largest such global exercise of its kind to date, an earlier series of "Quantum Dawn" exercises (the latest being Quantum Dawn V)[2] tested similar controls and financial organizations on a smaller scale.

Organized by SIFMA, which is the voice of the United States's securities industry,[3] Quantum Dawn V "enabled key public and private bodies around the globe to practice coordination and exercise incident response protocols, both internally and externally, to maintain smooth functioning of the financial markets when faced with a series of sector-wide global cyberattacks. The exercise helped identify the roles and responsibilities of key participants in managing global crises with cross-border impacts. The exercise scenario emphasized cross-jurisdiction communication and coordination between member firms and regulatory agencies in North America, Europe, and Asia. . . ."

In the exercise press release after the 2019 Quantum Dawn V global exercise, the following lessons learned (recommendations) were noted for the financial industry:[4]

- Create a Directory of Critical Stakeholders and Key Contacts:
  - Creating a directory of financial services firms and key trade organizations, regulatory bodies, central banks, and government agencies that would respond to a global cyber or physical event is a good first step for the industry.
- Conduct Periodic Exercises:
  - The industry should schedule regular touchpoints and exercises. These exercises could be a catalyst for developing global information sharing capabilities and incident response and recovery protocols for critical public and private sector organizations and contacts.

- Enhance Information-Sharing Capabilities:
  - Enhancing existing information sharing networks, with organizations that currently manage crises in their respective jurisdictions, is key to building stronger cross-border information sharing between the public and private sector.

THE IMPORTANCE OF CYBER EXERCISES

Why spend time, money, and other resources on your organization's cyber exercises. What is truly at stake?

To gain a glimpse at the scope of the challenges faced by public and private sector organizations, the January 14, 2021 "DHS Strategic Action Plan to Counter the Threat Posed by the People's Republic of China"[5] report reveals quite a bit.

Following are a few small excerpts, but the entire report is worth reading:

> *In an increasingly digital and interoperable world, we face expanding threats to our cyber networks and critical infrastructure in scope, scale, and frequency. The Department's Components, led by the Cybersecurity and Infrastructure Security Agency (CISA), are acutely aware of these risks, particularly those emanating from the PRC. While CISA plays a central and cross-cutting role across our Nation's critical infrastructure, the Transportation Security Administration (TSA) and U.S. Coast Guard (USCG) also play a key role in bolstering resilience to cyber and emerging technology vulnerabilities in the transportation sector. . . .*
>
> *CISA maintains a close and collaborative partnership with industry tailored to bolstering cyber-mitigation practices against adversaries, from nation- and non-state actors alike. This unique private sector partnership approach enables CISA to disseminate*

cyber-threat information, host training, and personnel exchanges, and circulate threat bulletins and alerts. Recent products have included spotlighting PRC-affiliated cyber threat actors targeting U.S. government agencies, PRC malware variants used to attack and maintain a presence on U.S. victim networks, as well as targeting and attempted network compromise of healthcare, pharmaceutical, and research sectors working on the COVID-19 response and vaccines. . . .

Increase Resilience of the Homeland to Nation-State Threats: *Critical Infrastructure Assessment: DHS PLCY will bring together FEMA, CISA, and other key DHS Components to understand the potential impacts associated with PRC threats to critical infrastructure and assess any gaps in current DHS National Preparedness and Planning activities. Expand Homeland Partner (FSLTT and Private Sector) Threat Trainings and Exercises CISA and FEMA will augment cyber and physical trainings and exercises with FSLTT.*

CISA and FEMA will augment cyber and physical trainings and exercises with FSLTT and industry partners to strengthen the resilience of critical infrastructure targeted by the PRC. This includes incorporating PRC Tactics, Techniques, and Procedures (TTPs) and other "real-world" nation-state scenarios into large-scale cyber exercises, including Cyber Storm VII and Cyber Storm VIII. . . .

The Spring 2021 Colonial Pipeline and JBS Foods events showed the world what a failure to protect critical infrastructure looks like. Cyber exercises strengthen cyber preparedness in the public and private sectors by offering solutions that mitigate these very real threats.

HISTORY OF CYBER STORM EXERCISES

Just as military, police, and fire professionals have trained over the centuries in various scenarios, a new push to test cyber defenses began two or so decades ago at the U.S. Department of Homeland Security. Shortly after the formation of the agency, accelerated efforts began to look at critical infrastructure protection (CIP) in many industries, and the significant cross-cutting nature of cybersecurity was recognized with the addition of Cyber Storm.

If you visit the Department of Homeland Security's website at www.dhs.gov/cyber-storm, you will find the following description of Cyber Storm exercises:

Cyber Storm, the Department of Homeland Security's (DHS) biennial exercise series, provides the framework for the most extensive government-sponsored cybersecurity exercise of its kind. Congress mandated the Cyber Storm exercise series to strengthen cyber preparedness in the public and private sectors. Securing cyber space is Cybersecurity and Infrastructure Security Agency's (CISA) Cybersecurity Division's top priority.

Cyber Storm participants perform the following activities:

- *Examine organizations' capability to prepare for, protect from, and respond to cyber attacks' potential effects;*
- *Exercise strategic decision making and interagency coordination of incident response(s) in accordance with national level policy and procedures;*
- *Validate information sharing relationships and communications paths for collecting and disseminating cyber incident situational awareness, response and recovery information; and*
- *Examine means and processes through which to share sensitive information across boundaries and sectors without compromising proprietary or national security interests.*

Each Cyber Storm builds on lessons learned from previous real-world incidents, ensuring that participants face more sophisticated and challenging exercises every two years.

The portal also offers the reports from each of the previous Cyber Storm exercises, including an executive description, goals and objectives, participants, scenario, and an exercise final report.

In a 2018 blog post by Jeanette Manfra, the former Assistant Director for Cybersecurity for the department's Cybersecurity and Infrastructure Security Agency (CISA), the importance of cyber exercises is highlighted:

Cyber threats to government networks and other critical infrastructure are one of our Nation's most pressing security challenges. Consequences from attacks threaten the safety and security of the homeland, our economic competitiveness, and our way of life. With the majority of critical infrastructure owned and operated by the private sector, securing cyberspace is only possible through close collaboration, what we described as a "Collective Defense" model of shared responsibility.

Exercises are critical to testing this coordination, and more importantly, to building and maintaining strong relationships among the cyber incident response community. Carried out regularly, these exercises allow us to achieve solutions to some of the biggest challenges facing the homeland as well as raise the overall profile of cyber events and cyberattacks. . . .[6]

We recommend that anyone involved in cyber exercise planning read through the Cyber Storm final reports that go back more than a decade, including the latest report from Cyber Storm 2020.[7]

MICHIGAN PARTICIPATION IN CYBER STORM I

While Dan was the CISO in Michigan, the state was invited to be a player in the first Cyber Storm exercise, held in 2006. The technology and security teams from across the Michigan Department of Information

Technology (MDIT) worked with the Michigan State Police Emergency Management Division, the Multi-State Information Sharing & Analysis Center (MS-ISAC), the U.S. DHS, and several other states and federal agencies to prepare for many months – starting in 2005.

MDIT had its own internal incident response plans, strategic and tactical cybersecurity plans, best practice guidance from NIST and others, and the team thought they were ready to go.

But they were very wrong. The scenarios were deadly, and the team was not prepared.

The first two days of the exercise were brutal, with events that were (in hindsight) over the top: Explosions, such as terrorists blowing up one of their data centers and bombs going off all over town, left the team reeling. Almost all of their capabilities were quickly disarmed or taken away via hacked computers – creating a hopeless feeling.

By Day 4, the team was very tired and just looking forward to the end of Cyber Storm I and getting back to their day jobs. But there was one final task. They needed to get a Bull mainframe back online to process employee payroll and perform other essential tasks.

Why? In the scenario, one of the Bull mainframes was blown up, and the backup was rendered useless by a series of cyberattacks.

But how could they get the mainframe online? After temporary paralysis and puzzled looks in the team room, someone discovered the (simulated) phone number for Bull headquarters in France in the reference materials available.

Dan phoned this number, and someone with a thick French accent answered the phone. The conversation went something like this:

"Bull Headquarters, how may we help you?"

"Hi, I'm Dan Lohrmann, the chief information security officer for the Michigan government, and we have an emergency situation. We need a Bull mainframe (model xyz) immediately. Can you help us?"

"As a matter of fact, we can. We have one such mainframe left for sale."

"Great, we want to buy it. We know that we bought the same model for USD $12 million. . . ."

[After a long period of silence] "Our apologies, sir, but we have several other organizations that want this mainframe. The cost will be $45 million."

Dan put his hand over the phone, as he spoke to the exercise team in the room. "They want $45 million."

The room exploded with angry shouts: "What?!"

"Who do they think they are! That's extortion."

After some back and forth over the next 10 minutes, they negotiated the price down to $23 million, and the cyber exercise ended shortly thereafter.

But the next day, Dan's team held a "hot wash," where they went over the Cyber Storm I exercise with planners, several DHS monitors, and others who participated. They covered the good, the bad, and the ugly from the week, including lessons learned.

One staff member raised his hand and said, "The Bull mainframe scenario. That would never happen in real life. That was extortion. We were almost being held for ransom. No hackers would ever do that during a cyberattack!"

Someone else blurted out in a mocking tone, "Yeah. Ransomware!" as everyone laughed and agreed that this was ridiculous.

Little did anyone know that within a decade, ransomware (in different forms) would become a top cyberthreat. By 2020, during the COVID-19 pandemic, ransomware grew exponentially to become the top challenge for most technology and security teams in global enterprises.

Later, statewide cyber exercises in Michigan (and in many other states and countries) brought in the private sector to test hospitals and other organizations during a pandemic.

A 2008 article in *CSO* magazine discusses some of the takeaways from participation in Cyber Storm II.[8] Later cyber exercises blended in street protests and other scenarios, with utilities and other private sector organizations also testing their cyber response plans.

By 2014, testing of incident response plans brought in other components such as the Michigan Cyber Range and the Michigan Cyber Civilian Corps to test the Michigan Cyber Disruption Response Strategy.

CYBER SCENARIOS, EXERCISE PLANS, AND PLAYBOOKS

As mentioned in Chapter 2, NIST offers generous guidance in creating organization incident response plans for cyber emergency response situations. Another helpful resource is Mitre's Cyber Exercise Playbook.[9] This playbook covers tabletop exercises, hybrid exercises (including scripted injects [unexpected twists that are thrown into exercises] and real probes/scans), as well as full live exercises (including real and scripted events).

Helpful examples include:

- Master Scenario Event List
- Sample Exercise Incident Response Plan
- Sample Incident Response Form
- Sample Exercise Roles and Responsibilities
- Sample Red Team Event Log
- Sample Inject Observation Form
- Sample Master Station Log
- Sample After Action Report

CISA also offers extensive support via their National Cybersecurity and Communications Integration Center (NCCIC), which develops and supports integrated cyber incident response plans and guidance and cyber-focused exercises for governmental and critical infrastructure partners.[10] NCCIC's National Cybersecurity Exercises and Training conducts a full spectrum of exercises in cooperation with the public and private sector and international partners, particularly those who support U.S. critical infrastructure.

Additionally, the Center for Internet Security offers six tabletop exercises to help prepare your cybersecurity team for inevitable cyber incidents.[11]

HELP AVAILABLE, FROM A CYBER RANGE NEAR YOU

If you do a Google search for "cyber range," you will get over 400 million results, but a decade ago the "cyber range" trend was just beginning.

A cyber range is a controlled virtual environment where students can practice using their cyber skills without real-world negative consequences. From high school students to expert "white hats" with decades of experience, hackers can hone their skills and practice attacking and defending different systems in much the same way that a shooting range allows police to practice using firearms.

There are many state government cyber ranges, like the Virginia[12] and Michigan[13] cyber ranges. There are numerous private sector cyber ranges, like Palo Alto[14] and IBM[15] cyber ranges. In addition, there are many university cyber ranges, such as the U.S. Cyber Range hosted at Virginia Tech.[16]

But this was not so a decade ago. In Chapter 2, we described the Michigan Cyber Initiative. The Michigan Cyber Range was launched in 2012 as part of that wider effort after a meeting with Howard Schmidt, who was the Cybersecurity Coordinator and Special Assistant to the President.[17]

With support from the public and private sectors, the Michigan cyber team was encouraged by our meetings with representatives from the National Institute of Standards & Technology (NIST), the Department of Homeland Security (DHS), the Department of Energy, and others to create a first of its kind unclassified cyber range to assist not only in training and cyber exercises, but also in enhancing, cyber strategies, test tactics for teams working together in cyberdefense, and much more.

The concept was, and still is, in many cyber ranges, to test not only traditional computer systems, but also a wide range of Internet of Things (IoT) devices and virtually anything that connects to the Internet – prior to going live in the real world. Teams of technology leaders from within government, the private sector, and academia met with companies from around the state and country to encourage support of these cybersecurity efforts, and the response was very positive.

Cyber ranges are also available for virtual training and onsite to simulate various scenarios. The Michigan Cyber Range created cities, called Alphaville and Griffinville, to assist in the cybersecurity training:

Alphaville is an unclassified virtual training environment that resides in a high-capacity network. It is accessible from anywhere in the world and exists within a private cloud operated by the Michigan Cyber Range. Each location within Alphaville features different operating systems, security priorities, and challenges.

These locations include a City Hall, Public Library, Public School, Alphaville Power and Electric Company, and Zenda, a small engineering and manufacturing business.

This environment features:

- *SCADA*
- *Security Tools and Appliances*
- *Email, File Sharing*
- *Permission Management and Access Controls*
- *DNS and BGP*
- *Various vulnerable databases and websites*
- *Alphaville is configured and misconfigured to specifications*
- *Ability to be customized*

Camp Grayling is a brick and mortar town that the Michigan National Guard uses to conduct training exercises. Griffinville is a

3D virtualized representation of Camp Grayling built with Unity. Our plan is to incorporate physical PLCs such as water pumps, door locks, and electrical systems into Camp Grayling and tie them back to the virtual infrastructure back at Merit.[18]

INTERNAL BUSINESS CONTINUITY PLANNING (BCP) PLAYERS

In the military, continuity of operation plans is built into their ethos, training, and execution. Some of the best business continuity plans (BCPs) have come from those who have either retired or left the military and joined the public sector.

There is a military saying, "You don't exchange business cards during a crisis." One should plan ahead of time so that people know what needs to be done, and the different players who should take ownership of the different roles.

It takes time to do this organically within the organization and to identify all the players needed, from law enforcement agencies to third-party partners. Think of the most likely and relevant scenarios (e.g., what could potentially happen) and then build a plan of action around that. This group should include legal, finance, business leadership, the technology internal team, technology vendor partners in your supply chain, and potentially even key clients.

Businesses seldom take time to benchmark against each other in the same industry. However, in particular, those who are very successful have proactively reached out to colleagues who are in similar businesses. Although some might have the view that they should not talk to the competition, there is huge merit in opening up a conversation, exchanging experiences, and benchmarking their BCPs against each other.

Yuval Illuz is the group CISO and COO of Trust, Data & Resilience at Standard Chartered Bank, a global bank headquartered in the UK with the majority of its global business leadership based in Singapore.

He currently leads more than 2,000 employees globally across cyber security, business continuity, and operational resilience for the group. Within a span of 18 months, his team has had to manage the global pandemic and strengthen its capabilities in the face of growing cyberattacks and natural disasters like floods that could impact the bank, just to name a few. His other responsibilities include data privacy, analytics, data monetization, AI and machine learning, training and awareness, and third-party security.

Yuval walked through a key lesson of the pandemic when it comes to business continuity. "The pandemic teaches us that the path to an overall stronger cybersecurity is agility. This means having a more flexible cybersecurity architecture, helping our technology teams easily deploy the appropriate ICS (information and cyber security) controls as a significant portion of our workforce went remote over the past 18 months.

"It also means investing in operational resilience as we grow the trust and loyalty with our clients. Operational resilience refers to the ability of organizations and the financial sector as a whole to prevent, adapt, respond to, recover from, and learn from operational disruptions. And it means, sometimes, to even implement a multicloud strategy, which enables businesses to better withstand the next threat to business continuity and prepare for the multiplicity of unknowns as we progress."

Yuval referred to the Solarwinds and Colonial Pipelines cyber incidents, which remind us that we should never settle in our efforts to be prepared for such cyber threats in our organizations. Threat actors will continue to evolve with greater complexities and strike with greater impact.

We need to constantly be learning from incidents (internally and externally) even if they don't directly impact us. Yuval revealed a continuous exercise that he has implemented within the bank, known as the Near-Miss exercise.

"Running a Near-Miss exercise based on recent incidents (although we were not affected) has significantly helped us to identify areas of improvement and be better prepared for the next attack. These areas of improvement might relate to a missing action in our playbooks, a weak control coverage, a broken process, missing or not up-to-date policy, and more. This is a great opportunity to take a proactive action to uplift the resilience of the organization. Combining these Near-Miss exercises with continuous crisis management simulations will build a more resilient and cyber-ready organization."

Yuval adds, "In addition, ensuring a Resilience by Design approach starts by frequently planning and simulating the crisis and incident responses internally, with our critical third parties, and regularly identifying improvement opportunities. This is crucial to defending against new threats without compromising client experience and system availability. Balancing a user-friendly experience with the complex requirements of enhanced security practices is critical."

He concludes, "To be future fit, we need to adopt a 'thrive' mindset that recognizes that disruption is continuous rather than episodic and embraces disruption as a catalyst to drive the organization forward. In that, it's critical to remember that humans and teams led by humans can bring the degree of courage, judgment, and flexibility that is required in a dynamic environment such as we are witnessing and will for some time to come. To that end, let's focus on strengthening the 'human firewall' through training and awareness from the board down to the frontline, while increasing communications with our clients to keep them abreast, allowing them to stay vigilant against the fast-evolving cyber threat landscape."

DESIGNING YOUR BCP IN ACCORDANCE WITH YOUR COMPANY'S MISSION

Preston D. Miller, CISO at NASA's Jet Propulsion Laboratory, has a great hybrid of perspectives. Previously, Preston was the Cyber Risk Information Assurance Manager and Incident Response Team Lead at the Washington Headquarter Services with the Department of Defense. Prior to that, he served in the U.S. Army. At NASA, applying the lens of cyber risk to the world of scientists and space, he had to adapt his thinking accordingly.

Coming from the Pentagon, they supported the warfighters, and "C – Confidentiality" was at the top of the triad "CIA." "Can we relay messages and assure confidentiality around those messages and operations?" By ensuring they had encryption and operational security, everything they were implementing leaned toward confidentiality.

When Preston transitioned to NASA, he quickly realized that security was done differently there. "I ran into a bit of a culture shock," Preston explained in a *Mega C-Suite Stories*[19] recording. "The main business of NASA is to share information, science, and data with our external partners, to build spacecraft to land on planets like Mars; overall, to just advance the community's understanding of the universe and the solar system, which is a very different objective from supporting the warfighters.

"In my world at NASA, 'I – Integrity' is at the top of our list. It's not so much that we are trying to keep the data that we are sharing safe, but can we trust the data that we are sharing back and forth between our communities, and can we trust the data that we are sending back and forth to our spacecraft and operations?"

Preston had to adopt an entirely different mentality of how NASA defines risk, its primary concerns from a cyber risk perspective, and how to communicate with the business leaders around cyber risk. This is first about understanding the risk thresholds and the risk appetite of the core business units, which involves sitting down with the business leaders, system engineers, and project managers of space operations to learn what they care about and what they identify as risk to their mission. Then he must figure out a way to communicate risk in the same language. "One of the things I found out earlier on that tripped me up is that I had to work out some of those language barriers; what the business meant by significant risk is very different from what I meant by significant risk."

Preston had to change his conversation and convert the risk for one particular business leader: "That old platform that you're using in one of the legacy space operations has a direct tie to this mission-critical system. And if we take those vulnerabilities that we found there, here's how an attacker can exploit those things to get access to that mission critical system. That can mean mission failure for you."

Preston explained how he has been on a campaign to change the cybersecurity office from the office of "no" to the office of "know." "Are we informing our end users of the right security principles, processes and procedures? Are we the office that they can rely on as a strategic partner at designing secure operations and systems? We want to give you the tools, the information, to design secure spacecraft and systems because we want to be an enabler to your mission success." That comes with building trust, which creates an open space of having that conversation.

With NASA spending more than half a billion dollars on its space exploration efforts, it is important to be able to restore critical operations in a timely fashion. Having a robust disaster recovery plan and a carefully designed BCP is extremely important. At a minimum, it should be done on a yearly basis. However, for the mission-critical applications that would significantly impact the business, you might run your BCP more regularly, perhaps every quarter, even if it's just a tabletop exercise, to make sure the business-critical applications and services are well-tested and resilient. "Having a muscle memory for your business admin to know what to do in case of an event is really good."

Preston's final piece of advice? "We may know our craft inside and out, but that does us no good if we can't tie that back to make the business successful. Be ready to listen to our business partners. People don't care how much you know until they know how much you care. Show that you care about their business, you care about their success, and I think that will pay many dividends for you and your endeavors as a security professional."

In general, what does a good BCP look like for most businesses?

- Setting up a mini crisis action team.
- Doing a walkthrough with the players to see when (the conditions) and how the executive team will be notified.
- Playing out the scenarios and tracking the time it takes to go down all the different checklists.
- This exercise will also reflect the time it takes to go up the chain of command, and for the board and executives to have made the decisions that they need.

As part of their training and exercise programs, there are some companies that have engaged professional media consultants/TV reporters to role-play with their spokespeople and train them in articulating crisis issues. This will help you gauge the quality and effectiveness of your training. The nonappointed spokespeople should also be trained to direct the media to the spokespeople who have been equipped specifically to answer questions.

Finally, board education needs to include cybersecurity awareness. Some board associations (e.g., the North American College for Corporate Directors and the American College for Corporate Directors, who both provide education and credentials for boards of directors) have now incorporated cybersecurity training into their certification programs.

WHERE NEXT WITH YOUR BCP?

Practice makes perfect. Once the BCP is completed, the next step is to rehearse it and test it. Doing a walk-through tabletop exercise with everyone who is involved in the execution of that plan is incredibly important.

Legendary U.S. football coach Vince Lombardi once said, "Practice does not make perfect. Only perfect practice makes perfect." A perfect practice of your BCP requires the involvement of your executives and the board of directors in the actual exercise. Boards and executives across all levels should recognize that their organization is a target and they need to be prepared to respond fast and well in times of crisis. When boards are invested themselves, putting their hand up to engage in these exercises, there will be less doubt about their roles should the business be breached, or appear on the news headline.

As a result, the organization's ability to recover quickly is strengthened. The most mature companies are those that invest the time to run these exercises, provide expectation training from the top down, and are committed to improving their BCPs with continual drills.

HOW OFTEN SHOULD WE BE RUNNING OUR BCPs?

Several CISOs shared their views of the frequency of these drills, and all highlighted that short and weekly drills are valuable for the technical team. This ensures that the staff maintains their qualification and sharpens their skills and ability on performing their tasks in accordance with the different crisis scenarios, and within a specified timeframe.

For a much broader operational testing, the security operations center (SOC), for example, is worth running SOC testing at least once a month, and even perhaps once a week if a company has the bandwidth.

For CxOs and the board, running a tabletop exercise annually with the crisis action team is crucial. Companies that are high on the learning curve generally do them twice a year.

AUTOMATED RESPONSES TO INCIDENTS

We close this chapter with a brief story that was sent to us by Arden Peterkin, who manages a complex K–12 environment for one of the largest U.S. school districts, with over 100,000 endpoints. Arden is the district's information security officer, and he urged us to highlight the ability to automatically respond to many security incidents in real time.

Arden's security team acquired a security orchestration automation and response platform (SOAR) capability, internally referred to as the "Robot," to prepare for what they believed would be increasingly persistent ransomware attacks. The robot was programmed to provide 24/7/365 monitoring of their data centers and endpoint systems. It would eliminate the dependency on human intervention to diagnose and respond to critical security events in a timely manner. And, because of the short interval between infection and ransom demand, the robot was programmed to act on perceived threats within three minutes or less.

This approach has been very successful for the school district. They have had 16 observable ransomware occurrences that were mitigated without human intervention, within three minutes, with no noticeable impact. In almost all cases, the events were triggered by phishing emails. Thankfully, they have had few to no instances of false detections or isolations due to ransomware's unique characteristics.

It is because of these and other cyber defense strategies currently in place that the school district is prepared to sustain, monitor, and improve their cybersecurity posture during these challenging times.

CHAPTER 4

What a Leader Needs to Do at the Top

Great persons are great because of good, strong foundations on which they were able to build a character.

—Alfred Armand Montapert

Most CISOs spend more time focusing on being a security technologist than a security executive. "Do you know how your company generates revenue? Who are the people in charge of the different lines of business? Why does your company have a security program? How are you working with your executive leadership? How are you adding value? Why do you even want your job? Is it a passion?" Steve Katz, widely recognized in the industry as the world's very first CISO, emphasized the importance of any security leader knowing the answers to these questions.

This chapter reviews many key lessons Steve and other leaders shared in different sessions of Shamane's "Mega C-Suite" series with her Cyber Risk Meetup global community,[1,2] as well as leaders she spoke to specifically for this book. Cyber Risk Meetup[3] is a platform founded in 2017 to facilitate the exchange of knowledge sharing across industries and thousands of international experts have engaged with it since then.

BUILDING RELATIONSHIPS WITH YOUR BUSINESS LEADERS

It is important for CISOs and security leaders to meet with executive business leadership regularly. If the only time they see you is when there is a problem, then they associate you with the problem.

SPEAK THEIR LANGUAGE

Do CISOs really know the top few things that the board is interested in?

In Shamane's conversations with board members, they highlighted what they would like to hear during presentations:

- What are the current hot topics?
- Is there enough talent or resources for the CISO to do his or her job?
- Looking ahead, is the company focusing on the right things?
- How is the company doing compared to its peers? Better, worse, or the same?

Board members are not interested in the detail matrix (e.g., the number of pings, viruses, and vulnerabilities). Boards may consist of CEOs or members of other company boards, and they will tell you what those organizations are doing, what they are doing better, or as well as, and why they are doing this differently here or not at all. In the end, what they would like to know is: As the risk posture changes, are we improving, and if not, why?

Telling the board "we stopped 8,700 attacks" does not mean anything. In presenting to the board, any piece of information needs to have a meaningful "so-what" attached to it. If there is no reason for some information to be there, then do not include it. Always anticipate the "so-what" for any statement or statistics to be included in the deck. If the reason the information is there is just to tell the board how smart you are, they will not appreciate it.

Albert Einstein said, "If you can't make it simple, you don't understand it."

Steve Katz also said, "If you are hungry, you don't care how a sausage is made. You just want something that tastes good."

Every C-suite and board member believes they are smart. If they do not understand what you are saying in a presentation, they assume you are not competent enough to explain it well and are wasting their time. In speaking to the board, always question yourself and the statements you are making. Ask yourself, "So what? Why should they care? Why is this important?" People need to understand the *what* and *why* of what they are doing before you get to the *how*.

Steve highlighted a meeting at the National Association of Corporate Directors (NACD) where the CIO presented. He was quite happy sharing the results of his company's vulnerability management process where they patched most of their major devices except six of their most critical ones because they did not want to bring down the company.

"So . . . our six most critical devices are still vulnerable, is that right?" a board member asked. "Yes," the CIO said. "Then maybe you better go out and rethink your presentation. Because if our most critical devices are vulnerable even after a planned remediation, what's going to happen to us with an unplanned attack?"

The CIO had not understood the business impact of what he was saying.

LAYING THE GROUNDWORK

Another piece of Steve's advice to this generation of CISOs is, "The problem with our CISOs of today is that they have not been confident enough to lay the groundwork in the beginning that they will never be 100 percent successful. Everyone runs the risk of being fired; if they're going to be fired, let it be for doing the right thing and not the wrong thing."

Steve shared a story from the 1990s of a bank that spent a lot of money leading up to a product launch. Just a month before going live, Steve was called in to look at security. Marketing and media were all ready to go, but he said no. The business leader told him that this would not stop them, so he had to explain that by doing so, they would be putting the company at risk.

The product was delayed by almost six months, and when it was finally launched, it went out successfully. Steve was willing to get fired for doing his job. "If I hadn't done it, I would have been fired for not doing my job," he explained. Despite reporting to the business leader at that time, Steve was able to establish credibility, as he reported to the board every quarter.

SECURITY VARIANCE

When Steve first joined a financial bank, he found that his executive assistant would always come in with a huge stack of papers for his approval; he decided to initiate a new policy called the security risk acceptance document. This was a simple one-pager that listed the policies that the business felt it could not comply with, the reasons why, and the risks as understood by the business leader. He also instituted a new line at the bottom to indicate whether implementing the policy was against the recommendation of the CISO.

These two metrics would go to the board; one would show which risks were accepted by the business, and the other which were against the recommendation of the CISO. No one ended up moving ahead, as it was a tricky position to stand in front of the board to say they knew more about security than the CISO.

THE FUNDAMENTALS AND TOP MITIGATION STRATEGIES

In today's digital world, data always remains extremely important. Data has tangible value (e.g., health records have value) and with it, the money associated with it. Every company becomes a huge technology pipeline.

In any dealings with a company, there is a trust commitment with you. As security leaders, we need to be mindful of how we fulfill that trust.

Executives need to be switched on and start asking themselves the following questions:

- What data do we care about?
- Where is our data stored?
- Who has access to it?
- How is our data secured?
- How do we respond if our data is compromised?

The CISO should never lose sight of the fundamentals (e.g., effective access controls, configuration management, threat and vulnerability management, effective backups). The Australian Signals Directorate (ASD) found that four mitigation strategies as a package would have been effective in preventing at least 85% of cyber intrusions that involved adversaries using unsophisticated techniques:[4]

1. Restricting user installation of applications (called "whitelisting").
2. Ensuring that the operating system is patched with current updates.
3. Restricting administrative privileges.
4. Ensuring that software applications have current updates. The Essential Eight is an expansion of the Top Four which includes mitigation recommendations (such as administrative privileges restrictions, patching operating systems, multi-factor authentication and regular backups).[5]

Without a solid foundation, the house will collapse. Likewise, you need to install locks and alarms before buying other tools such as infra-red sensors. Some security leaders have been known to chase after shiny tools and invest thoroughly in the latest technology. However, most of the time, looking after the basics would have addressed many main issues.

SECURITY NEEDS TO HAVE A BUSINESS PURPOSE

It is also important that security leaders not overrely on technology. Cybersecurity is not just about technology, but also about the process and people.

Successful CISOs are those who knit those all together and ensure that technology complements the process and that people are equipped with the right training.

Tiago Ferreira, a former agent with the Australian Federal Police and an investigator at Interpol, observes, "Being innovative doesn't mean applying new technology. In order to adapt and combat the ever-changing criminal landscape, first you need to identify the root cause of the problem and prototype the solution, then you apply technology.

"Technology is only a catalyst, not the solution. If you don't have the right solution, all that the technology is going to do is build more silos, create duplication of effort, and gather an increasing amount of data that will be difficult for the human mind to process."

Before deciding on a new technology, always consider the people and process elements as well. Do you have trained people supporting it? Is the right process in place that will help the business thrive? You do not want to introduce a new technology that will be seen as a hindrance or become a stumbling block to your users or your operators.

Plan for:

- Obsolescence
- Depreciation of assets (including people, processes, and technology)
- Recapitalization
- Appreciation of cybersecurity assets
- Continuous professional education

There have been too many organizations and CISOs who have not done this.

Information security is not just a technology problem; it is also a business risk issue. If you are not addressing a business risk or a problem, then why are you suggesting a security solution/plan? Why should the company desire security?

Steve Katz shared his opinion on the title of the CISO: "A CISO should be a Chief Information Risk Officer. We need to be dealing with risk and resilience. Businesses are not interested in security; they are interested in business risk, and business enabling focus. Focus on that and risk mitigation."

The CISO role as a cybersecurity risk advisor should be in helping people be aware of what they are doing and why, and the risks they are undertaking. Although they give advice on risks, they are not risk managers.

In saying that, how does one manage and address risk? How does one make their company resilient in dealing with dramatic risk? If security does not have a business purpose, then it has no purpose being there.

FIGHTING THE INNATE NATURE OF A CISO

As much as it is in the CISO's nature to want to protect everything, do not try and protect everything equally. It is not possible to reduce the risk to zero, no matter what budget you have. You can only reduce risk to some degree. Information has value; however, we waste much time and effort trying to protect everything in the same manner.

Many organizations have failed, spending thousands of dollars trying to protect a hundred million dollars' worth of assets and spending the same amount protecting assets that are worthless. CISOs need to look at *proportionate defense*.

Pick your battles. A survey done by Nominet of 800 CISOs and executives from companies in the United States and the UK reflected that many (88%) are facing high levels of stress.[6] This has led to mental (48%) and physical health issues, relationship problems, medication and alcohol abuse (23%), and in some cases, eventual burnout. On average a CISO's tenure is 26 months before finding new employment.

Steve comments that the CISO job has not been defined properly, even after all these years. CISOs are trying to run after perfection. He likens this to a scenario where a molecular biologist of a large pharmaceutical company has been researching a molecular cure for a disease. They go through different phases of trials that might progressively cost a billion dollars in research. Even if the researchers fail at the third phase, they are not fired; it is part of the job.

Likewise, the CISO's job is to explain risk. They do not own the risks; they advise on the risks of taking path A versus path B. CISOs are also not called to be politicians – they are not paid to give advice on what the politically correct thing to do is. When people are focused on politics, the approach often turns confrontational, where it's an individual against the world. The role of the CISO is to give advice on what the right thing to do is. "Learn to be a diplomat," says Steve emphatically.

There is also the challenge of the "impostor CISO," a syndrome that plagues many new CISOs when they compare themselves to the rest of the C-suite roles that have existed for decades longer. Shamane is a TEDx speaker on the very same topic[7] and having had more than a 1,000 exclusive one-on-one conversations with high-profile executives, she is passionate about this: "If you truly understand the purpose and calling of your role – that your role as a CISO can bring about a deeply meaningful outcome – then you will be true to letting your voice be heard in the most effective manner, rising above any security stigma and criticism."

There is a time to make a recommendation and a time to make a decision. It is important for CISOs to be conscious of the timing and to choose their battles carefully. If the executives decide not to take a CISO's recommendation, don't take it personally. It is just a recommendation, where you can educate respectfully.

HOW SHOULD A SENIOR EXECUTIVE APPROACH CYBER ISSUES?

Cyber is a relatively new problem compared to terrorism. John Yates, Director of Security of Australia and New Zealand's largest retail giant, whom we first highlighted in Chapter 1, shared his views on the executive approach.

"People tend to get very uncomfortable with new problems. There has been a perception, although it is changing, that cyber is a technical problem and needs just a technical response. This is fundamentally wrong.

"So how should a senior executive approach cyber issues? The first and most important point is that cyber is a whole-company issue and not merely a technical issue.

"If you leave it in the hands of only the technical side of the business, you will likely not get traction, and you may even be trying to solve the wrong problem. Cyber risk is a whole-company issue and it must be based on the threats which your company faces."

The second fundamental issue is that any response must be based on a full understanding of the problem and it evolves. Intelligence is key.

John highlights the importance of:

- Having a constant understanding of the evolving and ever-changing threat
- The agility required to pivot and change your plan/strategy in responding to threats

Take ransomware, for example. It is relatively new, so how should companies respond to it? Have they thought it through? Will they pay a ransom? What would the board's decision be? What would be the legal position in a particular state or jurisdiction? What would be the position on breaching sanctions, and what about the whole moral and ethical issues around paying criminals? These are questions for executives to constantly think about.

John explains, "The biggest skillset that I believe that I need in my business is the ability to influence and not alarm people. If you take an alarmist view, you can do that maybe once or twice. but if you constantly go to the board saying, 'It's awful, the world's falling in!,' people will start to question your judgment if the world isn't really falling in.

Yes, there might be fires everywhere but then you have to make a judgment on how to respond based on its intensity and ability to spread."

In explaining the problem, use plain terms. If you start using acronyms, numbers, or particular and technical means of patching or dealing with vulnerabilities, then people won't understand what you're saying, and they will switch off. They have to understand that the threat is not just a technology one but one that can be an existential threat to the entire business. As such, security needs to have a senior function positioned within the organization with access to the right people, not hidden in IT, legal, or risk departments.

For Scentre Group, their top two threats are terrorist threats and a cyberattack. A terrorist attack or other major incident in one of their Living Centres is their number-one risk. John believes that, awful though it would be, the business would recover from a physical attack relatively quickly, as it has well-exercised plans, great training and other processes, and the right level of engagement with relevant agencies and the police.

A cyber threat, on the other hand, could stop the business from functioning. If a customer's data has not been handled well and the recovery is painfully slow, this will result in a customer's loss of trust and confidence. John illustrates this with the potential denial of service or a ransomware attack example that froze their systems: "We invoice our tenants rent charges of millions per month, but we are now unable to invoice that. We can't bring in cash, which is our lifeblood, which means we would be in financial strife very quickly. Likewise, if communication systems didn't function then not being able to communicate with our centres across Australia and New Zealand would be a serious problem."

This only goes to show how easily a business can be paralyzed from a ransomware attack from which recovery would be difficult.

"Potentially, and this applies to almost every business, a cyber attack is an existential threat. And, if you haven't got a plan to respond, or, if you have a plan but it has not been exercised, then you are in serious trouble because neither your shareholders or customers would forgive you." John states.

When it comes to key roles to have in your security function, the four fundamentals for John are:

1. *Having good intelligence capability*

   This does not mean that you need to have 25 people. You can have one good person who draws on and gets support from multiple sources. If you're not basing your strategy and tactics on what the real problem is, then you have fallen at the first hurdle, because you're probably responding to the wrong problem.

2. *Having a strategic threat assessment*

   It is also important to keep the threat assessment up to date so you know the multiplicity of threats your company faces. For John, the range of threats are terrorism, cyber risk, fraud and corruption, insider threats, and protest. Every company has different threats that would be more relevant to them, but they have to know what they are and if they have changed.

3. *Having a control program for mitigation*

   This reduces the likelihood of being impacted. An effective control program can prevent an attack from happening. To state the obvious, it is all too easy to identify the problems. The challenge is in instituting developing and tracking programs to mitigate these problems.

4. *Having a great recovery and response plan*

   If an incident does happen, if you have not tested and challenged your response plan even though you've got all the controls, it's unforgivable. It's unthinkable for a board not to ask these questions.

Finally, be a detective. John shares that the prime function of a good detective is to be someone who suspends judgment, is curious, and does not make assumptions or jump to conclusions. Detectives don't make bold statements that can't be backed up with evidence. A detective constantly asks questions to assess the value of the pieces of evidence, challenge them, and then place the correct weight on them when found to be true.

Say to your business, "Here's the problem, here's the evidence that supports the description or analysis of the problem. Here's what I think is required to mitigate it, if you don't do it, this is what that is going to cost you, and these are the consequences."

John likens the discussion to court cases where you have an opening argument and then the evidence is provided, analyzed, and summed up for a decision point. It's very simple.

WHAT CAN THE BOARD CHANGE?

When asked for the top three things he wished boards and executives knew before going through a crisis, Theo Nassiokas, an Australian business-focused CISO, who comes with an extensive amount of experience in global banking and the intelligence field, shares the following:

#1. Boards need to stop using the technical complexity of cyber as an excuse for failing to adequately invest in cyber capability proactively. This is typically seen when CISOs are denied funding because they're unable to articulate the ROI, or quantify the value proposition or costs to be removed. Feasible cyber security investment should be seen as a business investment, not an IT issue, and as an investment in brand trust.

#2. Boards talk about innovation and digital strategies, yet typically remain focused on cutting existing costs. Innovation is about doing things better and smarter to increase existing revenues or realize new revenue streams and build ROI. Security should be seen as a core and proactive part of innovation; building trust into innovation is designing a sustainable reputation for businesses. Boards should put CISOs on the business decision making team.

#3. Boards and executive management need to be involved in cyber crisis simulations that are conducted regularly, so that they understand their involvement, and how effective the overall response will be. In doing so, the board should consider the role of cyber insurance and a strategic partnership with communications and law firms, so that they're prepared to respond to a high-profile cyber attack that would otherwise result in significant reputational damage.

STORY-BASED LEADERSHIP

As highlighted earlier, an important element of any good CISO is good communication skills. The challenge many CISOs have is that they got into the position by being brilliant technologists, which is a great skill and one of the best safety nets. The CISO, though, does not have that safety net. They have to build their future based on their soft skills (i.e., communication, negotiation, talking to executive leadership).

"If you look at any of the world's religions, the basics were passed on through fables," Steve Katz stated.

He also shared an experience of how a company demonstrated an antivirus product and picked up some viruses in the process. The next day, Steve had to speak to the board of directors. This was when PC viruses were relatively new. Steve had zero preparation and decided to go with storytelling. "Picture yourself down in the trading room and you are sitting at the terminal. You can only watch as the number five becomes an eight, and then the four becomes a three. What happens to your trading position?" Now, this was an image the directors could easily visualize, and they immediately asked, "Can this really happen?"

When you tell a story that is meaningful and one that business leadership can understand, they will want a solution. The board directors wanted to know if Steve could make the issue all go away. Instead of saying yes, this is where the CISO should clarify that they can only reduce the likelihood. The danger in security leaders saying yes is that they run the risk of losing their job if they promise something they can't deliver.

Instead of making a commitment you cannot keep, help your business leaders by keeping things in perspective for them. While explaining that you can reduce the risk likelihood for them, give your recommendations and explain why.

"Assuming you have done your job and met with the executives beforehand, when there's a breach, they already know who you are and what you've done to prevent it, and they know that it can't be avoided," Steve explained. "It's the same as a trader having their role expectation set; everyone knows that not everything they do will be successful. They might make an investment and if it does not yield a return, they will not be fired for that, as the ground rules have been laid out."

At the end of the day, you have succeeded as a CISO if your board is able to say:

- We understand risk in the context of our unique business and its objectives.
- We have confidence that risk is being managed effectively and that there is a process in place to continually test those assumptions.
- We have confidence that our security investment is appropriate to both known and anticipated risk.
- We have a high degree of confidence that we are crisis ready.

SETTING A SUPPORTIVE CULTURE LEADS TO CREATIVE SOLUTIONS

Never underestimate a healthy organizational culture; when management backs their team and supports staff-driven initiatives, it sends a very strong message throughout the company that is amplified organically.

This was evident in the same podcast session with Leong Boon highlighted in Chapter 2. When asked what he believed was a key success criteria for National University of Singapore's healthy security culture, his enthusiasm as he talks about the support he gets from senior management was undeniable. "Senior management has created this culture where cybersecurity is one very important pillar that supports the entire university. With that, we have various security awareness programs that drive this. We do this via face-to-face sessions, talks, roadshows, and fairs where we engage our staff and students to help them understand the latest cybersecurity threats, trends, and what they should be looking out for."

Leong Boon offers a sneak peek of what they have been up to. "We recently collaborated with one of the famous escape room architects in Singapore to develop a large-scale cybersecurity-themed escape room on campus. As part of this escape room, you're supposed to be going around to solve puzzles to reach the final destination and complete the mission. We find that this is going to be another dimension of creating security awareness; a little gamification and yet at the same time, putting another spin to how we can actually advocate cybersecurity awareness."

He also shared about the value that management placed on raising the next generation of cybersecurity-savvy youths. "We are actually coming into our third year of embarking on a bug bounty program. For the first year, we initially opened it to the students, and the second year, to staff and students – both of which had quite good success, with thousands of dollars of bounties being paid out. Why did we choose to do this, being also the first university in Singapore to do it? We feel that we should have a forward-looking mentality that we want to adopt – that we are not afraid to put our applications out there for our staff and students to test for bugs. If our staff and students can find the bugs, naturally it would mean that hackers could also find them."

He concludes, "Naturally, we would want our staff and students to find them and disclose them to us, rather than having someone actually exploit these vulnerabilities."

Traditionally, it has been observed that when companies start on a bug bounty program, people are generally reluctant to volunteer their applications. They are of the mindset "Why would I want strangers poking around in my applications?"

However, in this case, Leong Boon found that it is because of the support from senior management that the number of applications has increased over the years, which is positive. They even saw their nonteaching staff from their administration cluster participate in the program!

He went on to disclose, "In fact, in the second year that we did this program, we got some feedback from previous years that our staff and students would like to have a crash course in penetration testing, because some of them feel that they are interested, but they don't know where to start. So we got an external vendor to come in and do a series of penetration testing workshops for our staff and students. So in a way, even though they might not be professional white-hat hackers, they still managed to get their feet wet, which was another interesting angle that helped us push cybersecurity."

Leong Boon ended with this: "I personally believe cybersecurity is not just a technical subject or element. There's so much more revolving around the business, and around the human element. In order to capture the right attention from our business counterparts from senior management, it's important to engage them at that level, where they will be able to appreciate cybersecurity from that angle, rather than focusing on the hardcore technical controls that need to be implemented. We need to be going to them to explain what would happen to the business – for example, what would happen to the university's reputation if an incident were to occur or how the incident could occur in our environment – that would help them understand threats and the risks behind cybersecurity at their level. As a result, they would be able to give their inputs and their advice, and even support our efforts whenever we require their blessing."

Cyber Mayday: When the Alarm Goes Off

CHAPTER 5

Where Were You When the Sirens Went Off?

When it comes to crisis communications, if you always focus on building a relationship with your customers, fans, and followers, you will always find yourself communicating in the right direction.

—Melissa Agnes

Your network has been locked! You need to pay 30 million USD now! *The following was an actual real-life negotiation between a ransomware gang and a $15 billion U.S. victim company that was hit with a $28.75 million ransom demand in January 2021.*[1]

After a few rounds, the victim company counters with $2.25 million, which was met with a scornful response by the ransomware criminals, paraphrased here:

It is very funny to watch a few of your admins trying to install MS Exchange server in 3 days and can't do it. We have encrypted 5,000 of 6,000 of your servers. If we do some very simple calculations, your expenditure is like, let's say $50 per hour, or maybe you are even more generous, $65 per hour, so 24 hours spent to restore one server multiplied by the number of servers encrypted by us, that is like $10 million in just only on labour expenditure.

It is interesting to note how these ransomware gangs have found an effective way to communicate the financial impact of business interruption caused by their cyberattack and demonstrate how their victims will cut their losses by adhering to their demands.

They continued, "But don't forget that you spent all this time on installation and *oops* you can't even restore any data because it is gone for the next 1,000 years."

They added the time factor pressure at the end of the message, but also showed "some" mercy at the same time: "The timer is ticking and in the next 8 hours, your price tag will go up to $60 million. So either you take our generous offer and pay us $28.75 million or invest in quantum computing to expedite the decryption process."

When the company asked for additional time, the crooks countered by writing back, "I don't think so. You aren't poor and aren't children. If you f*cked up, you have to meet the consequences."

A day later, when the company finally managed to get the authority to pay $4.75 million, the extortionists agreed to lower their demand to $12 million, on the condition that the remaining amount be paid within 72 hours. After a few additional messages, they came to an agreement where the criminals "promised" that:

- They hackers would not launch any new attacks.
- The company would get the tool to fully decrypt the encrypted data.
- The hackers would completely leave the network and never target them again.
- The hackers would give the company access to the data to delete it themselves. The data would never be published or resold.
- The hackers would provide a full report on their actions: how they got into the network, how the attack was carried out, including tips for improving security and protecting against the penetration of other hackers.

The company ultimately paid an $11 million ransom, with the criminals assuring them that they would not attack or help anyone to attack their network moving forward.

This ransomware scenario is just one of the more ruthless cyberattacks but has increasingly become as common as other cyber attacks. Shamane recounts another ransomware attack of an Australian transportation and logistics company with operations in road, rail, sea, air, and warehousing.

THE STORY OF TOLL

It was May 2020. Toll Group, the logistics giant that operates an extensive diverse road, air, sea, and rail freight transport services across 1,200 locations in more than 50 countries, suddenly went offline. This was not the first time. In early 2020, Toll had suffered from a major cyberattack that devastated its IT systems.

After the first attack, business owners were increasingly frustrated about their untraceable packages and missed deliveries. Social media was full of people expressing their disappointment. This seemed like déjà vu all over again.

King Lee, Toll's CIO, shared his insider story.[2] King spent 26 years in the United States when he retired from GE Health and moved home to Melbourne. He picked a very interesting year to move back, as Australia had recently just come out of a major bushfire crisis that put a lot of stress on the whole country.

It wasn't long after the bushfire crisis that Toll experienced the first cyber incident, which was followed very closely by COVID and then the second cyber incident. King joined Toll one month after the first attack, and two months before the second attack. "If you have gone through a cyberattack, you wouldn't wish it on anyone else and Toll went through that in a three-month period," he said.

After the first cyber incident, while Toll was busy putting in place recovery actions and looking at securing their environment, the second incident happened. "On the fourth of May, we noticed that there were encrypted files in the system and there were ransom notes left behind on the server. Straightaway, we were hit by ransomware. What we did very quickly was to bring the system down in an orderly fashion, shut down the internet gateway so that if there were any viruses that were still in the system, they wouldn't spread to our partners and customers." King walked through their approach.

Our Number-One Focus Is to Contain and Protect Others

Toll engaged their crisis management process, put a business continuity plan (BCP) in place, and started communicating to their employees, customers, regulators, and the media. This was put in place very quickly to control the environment and to notify their employees.

For the following few weeks, Toll painstakingly worked to recover the whole system and bring their business operations back online.

In times of crisis, King emphasized that it is important to act very quickly the moment a cyberattack is identified. However, *don't panic.* Coordinate so your employees know what to do.

You need to have a plan ready, so that when an event occurs, you don't need to think about what you should be doing next.

Have a Crisis Management Plan

When it comes to cybersecurity, every company needs to have crisis management and BCP plans in place. Teams need to know how to react immediately and what steps to follow to put in the proper measures.

Since your system is going to be down, a quick assessment must be made to determine how long you will need to use your BCP. This is critical for your business operation and for your customers as well.

If the system is not able to return to operations today, customers need to know how long they need to wait. Your customers need to come up with an alternative plan for their business operations as well. This is why managing expectations and communicating very clearly is absolutely critical. You do not want to lose the confidence of your customers.

Stay in Control of the Crisis

To keep control of the crisis, present a plan with time frames. Communicate what you are doing. Even if your BCP is going to be in place for one to two weeks (which is a long period of time), if the business, including customers, know exactly what you are doing, this will give them a lot more confidence in working with you until everything is up and running again.

FINE-TUNE YOUR BCP

After Toll's first attack, they found that there were areas of their BCP that could improve further. Even today, they continue to work with all their customers to fine-tune their BCP to face new incidents in the future.

King shared some advantages of joining an organization in the middle of a crisis, or times of rebuilding:

"I came in with a new thinking. I was able to look at the whole situation from a new perspective and ask a lot of questions. Most of the time, our teams already have the answers but sometimes people will say 'oh, we didn't think of that.' Coming in with a fresh pair of eyes is good.

"Most of the time you will find that the team already has a lot of knowledge and the know-how to deal with the problems. It's just about helping them to connect the dots and motivating them along the way," King recalled.

CYBER CRISIS IN PANDEMIC TIMES

Have you ever tried dealing with a crisis in a pandemic, which is a crisis itself?

"I joined Toll at the beginning of March [2020], and by the end of March, most of the staff are already working from home due to COVID. I didn't have a chance to meet with a majority of my team, business stakeholders, and colleagues, not just in Australia, but globally. I haven't even met them on video yet but I had to very quickly get to know the individuals well, the roles that they play, the whole organization structure and a lot of the internal process. That's a challenge for someone new to pick up very quickly," said King.

It is important to know your team and your colleagues well, as they know the background, history, environment, network, process, and the people. King breaks it down into three points:

1. Do a lot of listening. Have the patience to listen to what the team has got to say – their opinions and ideas.
2. A hundred percent leverage your team.
3. Work with your colleagues. Teamwork is of the utmost importance, and not just in a crisis. No individual can achieve everything by him- or herself. We have to work as a team to solve problems.

He went on to share three approaches that are helpful in dealing with a crisis:

1. Own your mistakes. Everybody makes mistakes, especially in a crisis time. We need to move quickly, make a lot of decisions along the way, and we are bound to make some mistakes big or small. Find an alternate way to move forward to agree on a decision. It's not about laying blame on others but focusing your energy on fixing problems and coming out with new ideas to move forward.
2. Be transparent with your team, your colleagues, and even to an extent with your customers and partners. Communicate what you know, what you are doing, and even what mistakes you have made. Transparency builds trust.
3. Communicate all the time!

King drew a comparison from COVID-19: "How many new cases do we have in Victoria, Australia, Singapore, and all over the world? What is the progress like with the vaccine? Where are we getting it?"

This is the information people want to know; from a personal standpoint, these are important to them. Similarly, in the midst of a cyber crisis, there is a huge demand for information.

- People need to know what is happening.
- Your business partners are questioning you.
- Your customers are looking for an answer.
- The media wants an update.
- Regulators need to be notified.

The big questions are: What was the exact problem? What are you doing about it? What are the improvements you are putting in place?

"The ability to communicate all the time, frequently, consistently, and provide the information to all the parties is extremely critical because if we do not communicate well enough, detailed enough, and clear enough, rumors are going to fill the void," King explained. Instead of letting people speculate, the best thing to do is to communicate what is happening.

MICROSCOPIC LESSONS – DAY ONE OF THE INCIDENT

On the very first day of Toll's second cyber incident, King gathered "the global business leadership, including the CEO, and discussed the plans and what we need to do next."

The first question on the top of everyone's mind was how the systems could be recovered. The expectation for Toll was that the team should be able to recover a lot faster than with the first incident, as it was thought they would have learned the lessons and have a better process in place.

It was a difficult situation to be in, but King asked the leadership team to look at things from a different angle. This was the second time Toll had been hit, which only proved that there are many actors out there waiting to attack them again. "We need to make sure that as we bring the system back online, it has got to be better, safer and stronger than before we went down."

The Mindset to Have During a Crisis

King explained, "Today we still talk about safety before speed. We need to be confident that as we recover our systems, we will be able to withstand and be able to detect further attacks because nobody wants a third incident."

Selling the Idea

"As much as it's very difficult initially to actually sell the idea, we had to explain to our customers why it was taking longer than what they expected to get back on operations and then continue to use BCP to run our operations . . . but I must say that our customers are very understanding. As I talk to their CISOs and CIOs, they agreed very quickly that this approach is right," King shared.

At the end of the day, even if an organization were to bring their systems back up, they would not have the confidence in reconnecting with their customers because they cannot guarantee that they are safer. Toll's approach was to share with their customers the reason for the delay and the measures they took to build a stronger and safer system so customers would have more confidence. They might have had to wait a little longer, but it was worth the wait.

THE RECOVERY

During the next few months, as Toll worked to recover from the cyber incident, they also worked closely with their partners in mapping out a cyber resiliency program. Toll had a program and was starting to run it; however, it was a 24- to 36-month program. The team had to now work out an accelerated version of it to execute over 30 projects in the next 12 months. It was an ambitious program. How would one prioritize?

King explained, "In every organization, you have to look at your own deficiencies or identify where your biggest gap is that you have to close first. The way we prioritize might not be the same as what other organizations need. For us, we want to make sure that our parameters are strengthened and build up a better defense. We want to secure our remote access with multifactor authentication and improve our end-point detection capability. We have enhanced our threat intelligence capability so that we can deal with any 'fire' before it even comes close to home. At the same time, we're building a much better detection and monitoring capability so that we can identify those threats early and terminate them."

IMPROVEMENT WITH HINDSIGHT

What went well? King remarks, "I would say that we've done a pretty good job communicating to all of our stakeholders. We communicated with our customers to give them information every day; when we have new updates, our accounts team will reach out to them and share the progress of what we've done, including answering their questions, consolidating them into a Q&A and broadcasting it to the rest of customers."

What could have been done better? King reflected, "We could have helped our customers to communicate with their customers. Although we were able to tell our customers what happened, their customers are also impacted by their capability as a result of Toll's cyberattack, and for some of them, they struggle in translating our communication in their context for their customer."

Every customer differs. In helping your customers communicate well, you cascade your message in a credible and effective manner.

King highlighted that despite expanding their call center by about 20%, the bandwidth still was not enough with so many queries coming in. They could have been better prepared if they had predetermined how they could scale up to double as compared to just increasing it by 20% or even 50%.

Toll had many employees who were not able to do much since their system was down. Some employees waited for information; others, especially the technology team, worked around the clock. King asked, "So how do we better balance the load and leverage our other employees? Although the skills and knowledge might be different, could we have leveraged them in our two-way communication? If we can do that better, then we will better help support the rest of our technology team as well."

THIRD-PARTY RISKS AND CYBER INSURANCE

The cyberattacks also led to a review of Toll's third-party risk management practices. Just as it is important to look within for areas of improvement, it is key to be mindful of the interconnectivity and correlation of your external parties. "Although there are things beyond our control, whether it is with our partners or systems connectivity, we've got to help them to help us," King explained.

Companies with manufacturing operations need to consider the gray area between information technology (IT) and operation technology (OT). The IT team might do what is required, but if the OT does not have the same protection and it is connected to the entire network, that is also another aspect of potential vulnerability to consider.

Cyber insurance is an additional layer of protection. Cyber insurance is just like any other insurance policy, which is a form of assurance. "Keeping in mind cyber insurance, just like any other form of insurance, providers will also ask you to continue to improve yourself, that you put in sufficient protection, and all of these contribute to lowering your premium." King shared. "So in a way, having cyber insurance also helps to encourage you to do the right thing. And I don't mean that if you don't have insurance, you wouldn't be doing the right thing, but this is just another push."

EFFECTIVE LEADERSHIP IN TIMES OF CRISIS

Leadership is crucial at a time of crisis. Here are King's top three tips for effective crisis leadership:

1. Stay calm. "The most important thing, especially if you're leading, and you're managing the crisis, is to stay calm because when the leadership team panics everybody else will panic."
2. Use the power of teamwork. "Teamwork is extremely important, because if you don't have trust and teamwork, you will not be able to mobilize everyone. You will not be able to synchronize your activities as well as possible, and it would not work as effectively. In a crisis, there's a lot of stress. Teamwork is absolute because you have to be really inclusive and patient to understand and work closely with one another."
3. Increase the level of ownership over the decisions you have to make on the spot. Engage people, take in their input, look at options available, and then make a decision.

"There's never going to be a perfect decision all the time. There's always going to be trade-offs, but you have to take ownership of those decisions. You do not want to procrastinate and say, 'If I make this decision, I'm going to be bearing the responsibility. If something goes wrong, I'm going to be blamed.' You just have to take ownership of that and make sure you've engaged enough of the discussion opinion but make a decision in order to act quickly."

A SUPPORTIVE MANAGEMENT HELPS BRING RESULTS

In earlier chapters, we explored key factors that helped a local university in Singapore come out of a crisis faster. It is noteworthy that Leong Boon, the head of IT Security, attributed the active involvement and participation from senior management during the crisis period for the quick recovery. "It was great that they did not point any fingers. Rather, they were really supportive in the sense that they wanted to find out what went wrong and resolve the issue there and then. It's entirely different when you have someone breathing down your neck with questions and assigning blame. The fact that senior management were very encouraging, also gave us the confidence that we have their support, and therefore, able to go into the investigation without fear."

Leong Boon highlights the difference this makes in establishing a healthy cybersecurity culture: "There's a top-down effect and if senior management is supportive of cybersecurity as an initiative that drives the entire University, then that would result in the staff, and even the students, feeling a sense of responsibility when it comes to cybersecurity. It's not just a pure function of the IT or security team, but what the entire university's culture has been set out to be."

The Global CISO and Privacy Head of Olam International, a major food and agribusiness company that is among the world's largest suppliers of cocoa beans, coffee, cotton, and rice, Venkatesh Subramaniam, is responsible for oversight of the entire security and privacy program spanning over 65 countries. Venkatesh previously worked at a leading U.S.-based mortgage servicer as their Global CISO and Business Continuity Head.

On his cyber crisis essentials, Venkatesh shares, "It will be very difficult to prevent all kinds of cyberattacks but it is vital that adequate attention is paid to technology and process controls for early detection and rapid response. Segregation, privilege access management, patching, and adequate rules to detect lateral movement are critical. Security orchestration and automation has now become part of basic security hygiene that facilitates automated triage and enrichment – this in turn will lead to accelerated investigation and response. Tabletop exercises and periodic compromise assessments are important sanity checks on incident management procedures.

"During a crisis, it is important to put together an 'A' team and a war room. External assistance to supplement the internal team would be valuable if the impact is high and hence as a proactive measure, it may be useful to have IR retainer models.

"The CISO needs to act as a buffer between senior management and the A team during a crisis – he/she should not put too much pressure on the team and burden them by requiring too frequent updates. At the same time, he/she should provide a higher level of abstraction to the management – with details around impact, containment, and support required.

"The CISO should also have predefined templates that capture details of an incident – this should be used while liaising with Corporate Communications and the General Counsel. This is to ensure structure, standardization, and completeness."

CHAPTER 6

Where Do We Go When the Power Goes Off?

Security Operations Centers Require People, Processes, and Technology Components

Remember, when disaster strikes, the time to prepare has passed.

—Steven Cyros

The lights began to flicker in the Landmark Office Building in downtown Lansing, Michigan, about 4:15 p.m. on Thursday, August 14, 2003. The leadership team was wrapping up the biweekly business meeting. When the lights went out, the 15 men and women in the room sat in stunned silence.

Downtown streets quickly filled with people scurrying around, wondering what was happening and how to get home. Getting out of the parking garage became a 30-minute challenge in accident avoidance. Several commuters volunteered to direct traffic on busy street corners.

Cell phones either didn't work or were constantly busy. The real shock came with a radio announcement that the entire northeastern United States, including New York City, was experiencing a blackout. No one knew the cause. Was this another 9/11? Could this be a terrorist attack? What was going on?

ASSESSING THE SITUATION

As Emergency Management Coordinator for the Michigan Department of Information Technology (DIT), I (Dan Lohrmann) reported to the State Emergency Operations Center (SEOC), which was on generator power. As I walked into the underground facility, I thanked God we had run three emergency exercises in the past five months to prepare for moments like these. On arrival, I learned the full scope of the outage in Michigan and surrounding states. My job was to coordinate actions with other departments and ensure that the DIT provided computer and communication assistance needed during the emergency.

I immediately contacted our DIT emergency coordination center, which was activated at our backup data center location – also running on generator power. Many of our technical staff and emergency contacts were on vacation, but after working through wrong phone numbers and unanswered calls, representatives from every section of the DIT were connected into our phone bridge. This line was buzzing with activity for the next five days.

The SEOC quickly filled with emergency management representatives from all parts of state and local government, the Red Cross, and the energy companies. Governor Jennifer Granholm and her executive staff also were there. Slowly the activity in the room started to build as phones rang, and meetings and informal discussions formed.

An executive update was given by each organization every few hours. The governor walked around the room to hear each report and ask follow-up questions. I was impressed by her focus and hands-on approach to the crisis. During one of the briefings, President Bush called the governor to promise federal support.

Over the next several days, our Public Service Commission (PSC) representative gave regular reports about the power outage's expected length in different areas. Maps on the walls showed which areas were still without power and which were still in a state of emergency. A pattern developed in which power was restored quicker than estimated, but in some cases the power was unstable and failed shortly after it was restored, hampering our computer restoration efforts.

The biggest issue was water. Many organizations, including the National Guard and the Red Cross, helped get water to southwest Michigan. Private companies donated water and others volunteered to truck it in from one part of the state to another. Reports were given by the Department of Community Health on hospital coverage and other health-related issues. The Department of Agriculture was active in resolving food spoilage issues and restaurant food safety.

ESTABLISHING ORDER

On Thursday night, the DIT team faced numerous challenges and questions. Reports came from all over the state about whether services were up and running. Some computer servers went down when their uninterruptible power supply (UPS) failed. The Executive Office wanted to update the state web portal with regular messages from the governor and the Public Service Commission, but connectivity was down.

We worked much of Thursday night to get things working again.

Over the weekend, the DIT was involved with workarounds to get unemployment extension letters out, update benefit card credits (formerly food stamp allocations), and assist in coordination for many other business processes. At one point, the Department of Community Health couldn't get an urgent email to the Centers for Disease Control in Colorado. They thought their emergency center's generator would enable them to keep all computer services going in emergencies like these, only to find that their email server was in a different building without power. Situations like these continued to arise through the following Monday.

Power was expected back in Lansing around 4 a.m. Friday. Should state employees report? Since cooling for state buildings in Lansing was provided by the utilities via chilled water, not air conditioning, would the computer rooms have enough cooling to bring up servers in time? The decision was made to have Lansing employees report, even if computer networks were unavailable. Through the dedicated efforts of employees, most computer services were available by 9 a.m. Friday morning in Lansing.

In most of Detroit, power was unavailable until Saturday morning. Work continued through Monday morning as the DIT went through the same processes in Detroit that were followed in Lansing the previous Friday.

CYBER TEAMWORK DURING A BLACKOUT

Intelligence reports surfaced after the incident claiming that a computer virus or foreign nation-state hack may have triggered the Northeast blackout of 2003. It was (much later) determined that "overgrown trees" that came into contact with strained high-voltage lines near facilities in Ohio owned by FirstEnergy Corp. were the real cause.[1]

However, it is true that there was a cyber component to the outage: "a bug in a GE energy management system that resulted in an alarm system failure at FirstEnergy's control room, which kept the company from responding to the outage before it could spread to other utilities."

Nevertheless, regardless of the cause, the steps to respond when emergencies occur remain the same. An "All Hazards" approach means that whether natural causes (like tornadoes, hurricanes, and floods) or manmade causes (like a cyberattack or arson) lead to a crisis, emergency responders need to work as one team to coordinate actions and recovery.

No doubt, forensic teams within incident response teams in a cyber emergency will be busy identifying and (when ready) remediating cyberattacks, but when the lights and power go out, most of the rescue responses remain the same – no matter the initial cause.

STEPPING BACK TO STEP FORWARD

So what lessons did we learn? On the positive side, our previous exercises helped us. Having a common incident tracking system at the SEOC and DIT emergency coordination center was priceless. It allowed everyone at the department command center to see all the actions, alerts, logs, and issues available at the SEOC. We could share common event logs and track actions taken across the enterprise.

On the negative side, we learned that behaviors change when real emergencies occur. Most staff went home to check on their families before coming back to work. What if power had been off in all of Michigan? Would everyone have reported as quickly? We were amazed at how an extended loss of power affected so many other areas. What if the outage had been a week or longer? As a result, we updated several parts of our emergency plan activation procedure.

Looking back at the blackout of 2003, I realize again how vulnerable we are to emergency situations. From hurricanes to power outages to terrorist acts, we can prepare for emergency situations, but we can't control events.

For Michigan's DIT, the power outage enabled us to gain a more positive "can-do" reputation with our customers. Our relatively new department had now lived through an emergency with the agencies we serve, which helped build trust. Not only did the blackout strengthen the new relationship with our client agencies, it showed the tremendous accomplishments we can achieve through teamwork in our own agency.

Despite a hectic workload and an intense atmosphere, I was able to step back a few times to watch how things were running in the SEOC. I was amazed by the calm dedication and lack of panic. I was proud of the response everyone provided, and especially that our prior planning paid off. I'm proud of the excellence and teamwork we showed as a department.

The importance of people, processes, and technology cannot be overemphasized in cyberdefense efforts.

PEOPLE, PROCESS, AND TECHNOLOGY IN CYBER EMERGENCIES

How do these elements come together in daily practice? What does it look like when the phone rings and the person on the end says, "We have a significant cyber incident that needs to be escalated"? The following is a helpful story from an outstanding cyber leader: Texas CISO Nancy Rainosek.

Early in the morning on August 16, 2019, a ransomware attack on Texas entities began that spread across the entire state and impacted 23 local governments. These were smaller entities with little in-house IT knowledge or support. The Texas Department of Information Resources (DIR), the state agency charged with leading statewide cybersecurity response, was notified at 8:36 a.m. that eight local government entities had suffered a ransomware event. Over the next two hours, 11 more reports came in, and at 10:30 a.m., one of the municipalities reported that its Supervisory Control and Data Acquisition (SCADA) system had been impacted. This system controlled the monitoring and distribution of the entire local community's water supply. Given the number of entities impacted and the very real public health and safety threat, DIR notified the governor's office to discuss issuing a disaster declaration.

Shortly after 11:00 a.m., Governor Greg Abbott issued Texas's first statewide disaster declaration for a cyber event.[2] With the declaration, the Cybersecurity Annex to the Texas Emergency Management Plan was put into action. The declaration also activated the Texas Division of Emergency Management's (TDEM) State Operations Center (SOC). By noon that same day, the SOC was fully active on a 24/7 operation with state and federal incident responders. Leveraging the logistical expertise of TDEM, Texas held the first coordination call with all potentially impacted entities at 2:30 p.m.

Over the next two days, Texas incident responders identified, prioritized, and visited all impacted entities across Texas. And by the end of Friday, August 23 – one week after the incident began – all impacted entities had been remediated to the point that state support was no longer required.

Nancy Rainosek emphasizes that Texas's successful response to this unprecedented cyber event resulted in impacted entities being restored quickly with no ransom paid. The state's response cost one-tenth of the ransom demanded by the criminals responsible for this attack. The extensive preparation and cooperation between the responders led to the entities being back online and in the rebuilding phase within one week of the attack.

The following preventive measures also contributed to Texas' preparation for such an event:

- Disaster Definition: State legislation earlier in 2019 amended the definition of a disaster to include a cybersecurity event. Additionally, it allowed the governor to order the Texas National Guard to assist with defending Texas' cyber operations.
- Cybersecurity Annex to the Texas State Emergency Management Plan: In 2017, legislation called for DIR to create a statewide cybersecurity incident response plan. DIR coordinated the plan's development with TDEM, the Texas Department of Public Safety, and the Texas Military Department. DIR held incident-handling training and incident response exercises with partners to ensure the ability to quickly operationalize the cybersecurity annex.
- Managed Security Services Contract: Through DIR's Shared Technology Services, state and local governments can utilize a prenegotiated cyber incident response contract with a managed security services vendor with no retainer fee. All contractors under this service are background-checked in advance so they are ready to assist on demand. Through the contract, DIR established service-level agreements for guaranteed response times and service quality and delivery.

- State Operations Center:[3] Utilizing TDEM's State Operations Center was a key driver in Texas's success. TDEM was prepared to communicate with local entities through its district disaster coordinators and has critical tools to communicate with field teams. Additionally, local governments are accustomed to the communication channels from TDEM.

The other crucial key to Texas's success in this event was the collaboration and cooperation of state and federal partners. Per the State of Texas Cybersecurity Annex, DIR led the incident response effort. State responders included:

- Texas Military Department
- Texas Division of Emergency Management
- Texas A&M University System's Security Operations Center/Critical Incident Response Team
- Texas Department of Public Safety
- Other agencies providing consultative work
- Private sector vendors – both paid and volunteer

Federal responders included:

- Federal Bureau of Investigation (criminal investigation)
- Department of Homeland Security (observation and forensics)
- Federal Emergency Management Agency (observation)

The FBI teams worked well with the Texas responders and were quickly integrated with the other responders on this joint effort. They provided clear and timely information and were excellent partners on the forensic side of this mission.

Many private companies offered assistance during the event. DIR did not have the resources to adequately vet and train these resources, given the urgency of this matter. The Texas Legislature proposed a bill to strengthen the state's cybersecurity response through a series of measures, including requiring DIR to establish a volunteer incident response team, with appropriate background checks and incident procedures. This would help ensure that Texas is prepared for the next major incident affecting multiple entities in the state.

CISO MINDSET REGARDING SECURITY INCIDENTS

"I can tell a lot about a person's cybersecurity background through a simple discussion," says North Dakota CISO Kevin Ford. In his experience, many cybersecurity conversations involve high-minded ethical considerations around the importance of data. Most people fall into one of three groups.

In the first (largest) group, conversations go something like, "Who are these hackers, and why would they target us? Who do they think they are? They should be arrested!"

According to Kevin, these are generally conversations with new cybersecurity staff, noncybersecurity IT staff, or perhaps laypeople like reporters and legislators. The presupposition of this conversation is that any cybersecurity incident is intolerable.

Kevin continues, "The truth of the matter is, that in any sufficiently large period, or in any sufficiently large network, cybersecurity events will happen. The quality and effectiveness of your cybersecurity program only extends the time between events."

The second group's conversation is more nuanced around the concept of cyber risk. The cyber risk concept, broadly construed, treats cybersecurity as a series of decisions and actions around the evaluation of both the likelihood and impacts of cybersecurity events. The cyber risk concept is powerful because it accepts the inevitability of cybersecurity events and prioritizes the prevention and responses to those events. Cyber risk conversation generally focuses on the fact that only a finite number or controls and activities are possible, given a limited number of resources, and thus certain risk treatments should be prioritized over others.

Kevin says he frequently has cyber risk conversations with executives, finance, and other business people who have spending authority or business opportunities tied to information systems in this group.

The final group contains what Kevin defines as "grizzled veterans." This conversation is generally with experienced cybersecurity pros, and typically happens behind closed doors in CISO support groups. This group agrees that protecting data is important, and they assume that the correct risk-based decisions are made. "With these ground rules out of the way, we move on to discuss security operations," he said.

Kevin Ford's cybersecurity mindset and approach to cybersecurity were shaped by his impressive background. He helped develop the NIST Cybersecurity Framework. He served as the CISO and Director of Assessments for the private sector firm CyberGRX. Earlier in his career as a Deloitte employee, he worked on cyber policy development for the U.S. House of Representative and for the Department of Health and Human Services – Indian Health Service. Kevin shared his perspectives on security operations, the North Dakota Cybersecurity Operations Center (CYOC), information sharing, playbooks, and multistate operations.

DEFINING SECURITY OPERATIONS?

In the business world, the operations team designs and manages methods of production of a product. When operating as designed, the work associated with producing an organization's product runs smoothly and efficiently. However, due to entropy, there are evolving and recurring factors that sneak into workflows that disrupt production, causing organizations to redirect work to fix the issues. This unplanned work is deadly to organizations and inhibits their ability to deliver their product. Cyber events are a manifestation of entropy, the chaos that causes organizations to be less efficient and engage in unplanned work.

Kevin's goal as a CISO, from an organizational perspective, is to maximize the value of his team by reducing unplanned work for an organization. In this way security operations build value for the organization and are seen as a force for enablement. A team built on business enablement is an asset to the organization rather than just a necessary expense.

The goal of reducing unplanned work may sound crass in comparison to more high-minded ethical ideals, but the upshot is a more comprehensive and effective cyber risk posture for the organization. A public servant must be a good steward, not just of the people's data but of their resources. As such, the integrity and availability of state services for which citizens pay is every bit as much an ethical consideration as is the confidentiality of the state's data. This applies doubly for critical infrastructure like utilities and healthcare.

North Dakota operates one of the largest public networks in the world. Even on the best days there are cybersecurity events, the nature of asymmetric warfare against large attack surfaces. As such, it operates at a macro basis, and resembles a public health organization more than law enforcement. Success for the team looks more like a dip in the frequency and impact of cyber events than it does hackers in handcuffs. To accomplish this, North Dakota's governance risk and compliance team and secure infrastructure team make risk-based decisions to protect the network from cybersecurity events using the resources available. It is then the responsibility of the Cybersecurity Operations Center to reduce the impact of unplanned work on the cybersecurity events that aren't prevented.

MEASURING RESULTS: KEY PERFORMANCE INDICATORS

The North Dakota Cybersecurity Operations Center (CYOC) leverages specifically designed capabilities, skills, and tools to reduce the impact of unplanned work to state operations.[4] When a cyber incident does occur, the CYOC's aim is to mitigate the severity of the incident in an attempt to insulate the state from as much unplanned work as possible. Time is the key factor in reducing the severity of incidents. Key performance indicators the CYOC measures are the time it takes to respond to an incident and the time it takes to recover from an incident. The team considers an incident that is immediately responded to and recovered from to be a close second place to prevention of the incident. Team members identify that as response and recovery time is reduced to near zero, incident prevention and incident response and recovery are often indistinguishable.

The CYOC relies on Security Orchestration and Automation Response (SOAR) technologies to handle incident response at massive scales as well as to significantly drive down time to respond and recover from security incidents. The use of SOAR tools shifts focus away from human-based incident response and instead focuses on integrations to automatically respond to security anomalies.

As adoption of SOAR technologies expands across the North Dakota network, staff are increasingly shifting away from incident response to proactive content creation and development of security tools. Security analysts now focus on creating playbooks for SOAR tools that synthesize understanding of threat kill chains for identified risks, threat intelligence from shared feeds, and lessons learned from previous incidents.

As the CYOC increasingly integrates SOAR within its environment, human constraints to security operations are quickly dissolving and being replaced by constraints around information gathering and playbook development.

INFORMATION SHARING

The use of automation fundamentally shifted the operating model of the North Dakota CYOC. Before SOAR tools, even when the team could see a cybersecurity issue coming, staff were generally powerless to stop it due to the expansiveness of the attack surface.

As SOAR tools were rolled out across the network, staff developed greater control of the environment, and the reward for correctly identifying risk is greater than before. As such, cyber risk information such as threat intelligence, kill chain analysis, and environmental and vulnerability information are key to successful incident response and recovery. If an analyst can identify a potential risk, the lifecycle of the risk, and the areas of the network that may be impacted by the risk, the analyst can develop playbooks to automatically detect and disrupt the risk if it is actualized within the environment.

Within the United States, there are multiple resources that provide valuable cybersecurity information, including Information Sharing and Analysis Centers (ISACs), the Department of Homeland Security's Cyber and Infrastructure Security Agency (CISA), which includes the US-CERT, as well as other formalized information-sharing and response organizations such as state-owned Fusion Centers and Security Operations Centers (SOCs). Internationally, there are also many similar setups (see Free Cyber Incident Resources beginning on Page 193). While these entities are valuable for providing context around events occurring in the larger national ecosystem, much of the information they share is restricted, highly edited, and qualitative in nature. Because the threat briefs are tailored to the widest possible audience, they often require significant human interaction to make them actionable in automated systems.

Fortunately, there are systems that may be used for more automated threat information sharing. Such systems use standardized formats to share identified threats across a user base. Standardizations around communication improves the capability to ingest records into SOAR tools with a low degree of human interaction. Because the human cost of running automated systems is far lower than traditional methods, the capacity for threat information ingestion, event correlation, and incident disruption and response is far greater. With the human constraints around threat intelligence significantly reduced, the ability to protect the environment becomes a function of the amount of structured threat data to which analysts have access.

STRENGTHENING PLAYBOOKS

In addition to automated data sharing, SOAR technology fundamentally shifted the way the North Dakota CYOC operates. Incident response is among the most intensive activities within cybersecurity operations and carries with it a tremendous human cost. SOAR tools reduced this cost by executing predefined actions when certain criteria are met. The predetermined actions and the criteria for action are defined in a security playbook that functions similarly to application code. Because the playbook, like code, can be distilled into an artifact, it can be shared and improved on a collaborative basis much like code within a repository.

As the CYOC increasingly relies on SOAR tools for incident detection and response, the capability of its security efforts rely greatly on the throughput of its playbook development. As such, more so than in many other operations centers observed, the CYOC relies on agile methodology and DevSecOps concepts of continuous integration and continuous development (CI/CD) to outpace and outfocus the adversary. In many regards, the CYOC resembles a development team.

MULTI-STATE SECURITY OPERATIONS[5]

The CYOC's reliance on large amounts of cybersecurity threat intelligence and modular playbook development causes it to function in many regards more like a big data or development shop than a traditional cybersecurity operations center. To increase both access to threat intelligence and exposure to playbook development and sharing, the North Dakota CYOC partners with other states across the United States and hosts collaborative threat information sharing systems as well as playbook repositories in which playbooks for incidents are shared and refined.

The Multi-State SOC operates on multiple levels. At the most basic level, partners have agreed to share threat intelligence data in a specified format using the same system. This ensures that information about incidents that occur in one state are immediately made available to all partners. Playbooks that align to multiple incidents are also shared at this level on the CYOC's GIT repositories.

At higher levels, the Multi-State SOC incorporates greater operational partnerships than are available in other similar efforts. For instance, when experiencing a major incident, it is common within the state government to receive help from other state cyber programs through the use of preestablished agreements. The most prevalent of these agreements is the Emergency Management Assistance Compact (EMAC). EMAC is a compact that provides, under certain circumstances, a vehicle for multi-state Cyber Emergency Response. However, to activate an EMAC the governor of the state has to declare a state of emergency. The state may then receive offers of assistance from other states, and would have to reimburse them for their effort. This EMAC process can be extremely expensive. In addition, because there is no guarantee that skill sets are aligned or technologies are complementary, it can also be unwieldy and inefficient.

The Multi-State SOC operates under the principle that it is far less expensive to address acute cybersecurity issues prior to becoming emergencies. The MS SOC's operating assumptions are that more frequent multi-partner engagements with preestablished operational capabilities, lines of communication, and a firm understanding of every participant's competencies and capabilities prior to engaging in large collaborative efforts are far superior to infrequent engagements with nonfrequent contacts. As such, the Multi-State SOC enlists partners in every step of the program from development to incident preparedness. When partners have shown that they are receiving the full benefit of the threat information and playbook sharing, they are then welcome to engage in the higher tiers of the operation. In this manner, the automated threat information sharing and playbook distribution functions as a filter to reduce the noise within local environments so that human security analysts can focus on more acute security incidents.

CHAPTER 7

Teamwork in the Midst of the Fire

Coming together is a beginning. Keeping together is progress. Working together is success.

–Henry Ford

Maria Thompson is the Public Sector CISO for Amazon Web Services (AWS). The significant cybersecurity incidents she recounts occurred in 2020, while she was the award-winning chief risk officer (CRO) for the State of North Carolina.

One significant cybersecurity incident impacted a county and a connected city affected by two different strains of ransomware. Neither was ever able to identify without a doubt which entity affected the other. This was because once teams started investigating as part of the foundational forensics process, everyone quickly realized that there was a "relationship issue," meaning a lack of relationship between the two organizations. One entity refused to accept any support or allow the state's Joint Cyber Task Force (JCTF) to conduct forensics in the environment. Anyone who understands an incident response process or has worked in computer forensics understands the importance of identifying *how* an incident occurred. Having that understanding and forensic details allows responders to map the path of the hacker and understand the tactics, techniques, and procedures (TTPs) used in the compromise.

The incident began when Maria's agency was notified of a ransomware attack within one city. The typical response for the JCTF is to establish a scoping call with the victim organization to understand their level of impact, support needs, and risk mitigations in place, such as cyber insurance. The JCTF is comprised of the National Guard Cyber Response Force, state cybersecurity professionals within the Department of IT, Department of Public Safety Emergency Management, Fusion Center, Local IT Strike Team members – dedicated, highly skilled IT directors – system administrators within the local government, and federal partners in the FBI and Department of Homeland Security. This is the group that engages in every cyber incident. On occasion, based on the specific threat, the state cybersecurity team may include other impacted entities within the critical infrastructure sector to ensure that they are kept informed of the incident and the current posture.

On the initial call, the impacted city informed the state cyber team that they could handle the ransomware incident on their own. The JCTF then offered consulting services and an additional forensic review, with plans to launch a National Guard Cyber and the IT Strike Team onsite.

Within the next 24 hours, the local government emergency management team within the adjoining county informed the JCTF that their infrastructure was also impacted by a ransomware attack. This incident impacted thousands of workstations and hundreds of servers across both local government networks. Most importantly, this affected criminal justice, public safety networks, and health services systems in addition to administrative support systems for payroll and collections.

Because of this new expanded landscape, the JCTF decided to provide mutual support of "boots on the ground" to both impacted sites. The National Guard assets were placed on state active duty orders to support this mission from a forensics and recovery support stance. The IT Strike Team provided initial triage, infrastructure rebuild, and priority of restoration.

After the first couple of days, the JCTF damage assessment was completed. The leadership realized that additional resources would be needed to assist with the inventory, tagging, and rebuilding of the impacted endpoints.

At that time, the State had one of the only cyber apprenticeship programs for veterans within the country. These veterans were placed within various state agencies to hone and mature their cyber skills. With the number of endpoints that needed support, Maria knew bringing them onboard to assist would not only give the JCTF an extra pair of hands but build the apprentices' skills through experiential learning.

Partnerships were also key to the recovery of these environments. The JCTF ensured that the team conducted information sharing and collaboration efforts with any vendor partners that could provide support as part of the impacted parties' ecosystem. Federal partners such as the FBI brought a lot of in-depth knowledge around the particular ransomware variant, insights into what the JCTF could expect to see within the environment, and best practices for eradication and remediation. These details were key to the forensics that was ongoing.

At the end of the engagement, corrective actions that were taken included:

- Containment of the threat; termination of any connections that could potentially cause the infection to spread externally.
- Notified local government to be on guard for suspicious communication from either impacted entity.
- Segmented the network into three distinct areas: dirty, staging, and clean. Recovery efforts focused on rebuilding the core infrastructure, which included Active Directory servers, telephony services, and so on.
- Priority of restoration was given to critical infrastructure such as public safety networks.
- Partnered with the FBI Communications specialist to craft a standard media release statement.
- IT support was provided by giving health service representatives loaner devices to allow continuity of operations.

- The JCTF worked with cloud vendors to conduct forensics of the cloud email services.
- Threat hunting to ensure there was eradication of any residual or persistent threats.
- Wide-scale information sharing of all indicators of compromise (IOCs) identified at either location were deployed and implemented in blocks across the state. IOCs were made available within a week of forensic support.
- Implementation of a firewall between the county and city networks to prevent cross contamination.
- Engaged the local emergency managers at the county level to manage and provide logistical support as well as provide situational awareness.

The JCTF held twice-daily situational report calls to ensure all players and state leadership were kept updated on the progress and needs were being met for the teams actively engaged. As the State's risk and security officer, Maria was present onsite for numerous days to meet with the local government leadership and provide statewide visibility and support. Though the city was more resistant to assistance, the JCTF was able to provide a reduced footprint, guidance and technical expertise where requested and accepted.

This ransomware incident stood out from others because it was the combined second and third government ransomware incident that year in North Carolina. It occurred at the same time the COVID-19 pandemic started to take hold, and concerns for social distancing were strongly voiced.

On a more positive side, because of the pandemic, the networks were being rebuilt to support remote work requirements. Roughly two-plus weeks into the engagement, the JCTF had to start scaling down onsite resources, establishing remote support capabilities, and strategizing on a new support model. This added an additional level of complexity to the overall operation. Fortunately, by the time the edict for working remotely was made, the core infrastructure was far along in its rebuild stage.

This incident, however, was just the tip of the iceberg. The following week, after reducing the onsite footprint, the JCTF was alerted that three K–12 school systems and another city had become infected by ransomware attacks.

These new cyber incidents stretched JCTF resources far beyond their existing capability to fully support efforts in the same manner as before. The JCTF had to strategize on means to provide remote and limited support to multiple impacted sites.

This was a defining moment, in which Maria realized the cyber team's resources could become stretched too thin. The need to ensure that the JCTF leveraged available private and public sector support to the maximum extent possible was the only way the team could effectively respond to a true statewide disruption. Up to that point, the JCTF was successful in supporting all impacted entities with, at a minimum, forensic support. However, moving forward in cyber disruption planning meant that JCTF's deficiencies must be addressed.

A BIG STEP BACK – AND ANALYZING WHAT WENT RIGHT AND WRONG WITH THE JCTF PROCESSES

In 2020, the JCTF supported 17 ransomware incidents, each similar in that the attacks were largely attributed to an initial phishing email and stolen credentials.

With each incident it became apparent to Maria that local government entities are targeted because of the lack of resources being placed toward cyber. In some cases, there were numerous security tools that were alerted on anomalous activities but due to the shortage of cyber personnel, these alarms largely went unnoticed until encryption of the environment was noticed. The team also learned that in these engagements, the JCTF personnel must ensure a clearly defined exit strategy before engaging.

As harsh as an "exit strategy" sounds, the JCTF leadership was aware that some impacted entities experience a level of comfort in having the expert team engagement on a continuous basis within their environment. There were times the impacted entities were alarmed when the team attempted to disengage. While this did wonders for the JCTF team's ego, it did nothing for the skill development, education, and confidence of the supported local entity.

From a long-term perspective, it is important that, as the network rebuild is being done, this JCTF work is performed largely by the impacted entities' personnel. They need to understand the new topology and gain a level of comfort with the new operations, as they are primarily responsible for the long-term lifecycle management.

What went not so right? The JCTF thought they were prepared, based on previous ransomware incidents that they had supported. Additionally, the team made the assumption that most impacted entities would be willing and open to external support. This was not the case.

Maria saw resistance come in various forms. First was the need for independence from "Big Brother," as the State is perceived to be. Second, there is/was still an element of shame associated with being impacted by a ransomware incident, and third, past negative perceptions. These issues combined made for a perfect storm of denial of support.

Additionally, because leadership had not anticipated that the city would choose to go on their own, some incidents ended up with multiple forensic teams. As with any forensic investigations, if you have too many chiefs, anticipate dissenting views between teams.

The JCTF voiced concerns that the IOCs and the date and time of impact did not match their backup and recovery plans as recommended by the supporting vendor. Though Maria tried to persuade the city's IT leadership, the decision was made for them to move forward using their strategy and not the JCTF's. Because the State does not have any legislative authority over municipalities, the JCTF had no recourse but to voice the concerns and step aside in favor of their decision.

There were many things the JCTF did right; most notably, with every new cyber incident engagement the team modified its tactics, techniques, and procedures (TTPs). The team was built to be agile, with the understanding that they are always learning and need to be flexible to adapt and engage each incident uniquely. During this engagement, because of the separate but interconnected infrastructure, the JCTF was able to adjust, test, and fine-tune its playbooks.

As luck would have it, the State had conducted its first Statewide Cyber Tabletop Exercise a month before the incident. This exercise was attended by state, local, academic, and private sector critical infrastructure partners. The exercise facilitated discussions as well as enlightening those local government entities who were not previously educated about the cyber support provided by the State. Since then, the National Guard Assessment and Assist Team has conducted numerous TTXs for local government and academic institutions across the state.

These exercises were not only invaluable in building relationships across the state but increasing the knowledge, skills, and abilities of the local governments' IT staff. Lastly, the exercises played a crucial role in identifying "pockets of need" across the state, areas where more training and support were needed to increase the security posture and reduce risks.

Since those ransomware incidents, the JCTF has addressed other cyber incidents with far-reaching potential impacts, such as SolarWinds and HAFNIUM.

A PRIVATE SECTOR INCIDENT WITH A (SOMEWHAT) HAPPY ENDING

Earl Duby is the current CISO at Lear Corporation. Several years ago, when Earl managed the incident response team for a large financial institution, the CEO received an extortion letter via an anonymous public email account. The note threatened to release a large number of personal account records of bank customers unless a small amount of Bitcoin was provided to the extortionist. Included in the email was a sample of records, which proved the legitimacy of the claim. But they also provided their team with the first clue.

With the help of the fraud team, the forensics team quickly determined which system the records came from. Then, through log analysis, they figured out which accounts accessed those specific records and when. The good news was that they could determine which one of the bank locations was used to access the files, but still couldn't nail down the exact computers. The records were accessed with a generic account that is normally used for training new users in the on-site training lab (security finding number one – generic accounts that could access customer data). Once they were locked in on the training lab, and a general timeframe, the fraud team worked with Earl to start the detective work.

They reviewed security camera footage, looked at training lab sign-in sheets, and talked with employees. They discovered that the lab was also used as a break room and that employees could go into the lab and check personal emails and surf the web, which they could not do from their workstations.

Over time, the field of suspects was narrowed to a handful of employees. That's when the real fun started. Earl grabbed his black bag of forensics gear and caught a flight. He arrived at the site at 11 p.m., checked in with the front desk guard, and set off to image hard drives – a task that took all night. He then gathered his gear and caught the first flight home.

In all, Earl gathered a dozen different images from the desktop devices of a handful of employees. He didn't have much to go on. The team had a spreadsheet that was in the original extortion note, the email address of the anonymous extortionist, and a few hunches. The rest was all forensics, time, and periods of frustration. Painstakingly, each image was indexed, analyzed, and documented. Slowly the pieces started coming together.

At the same time, the company's fraud team was working on different clues, and Earl's cyber forensics team was constantly trading notes. The fraud team would find something in the data, and that would lead to a new search term in the forensic team's analysis. Eventually, the U.S. Secret Service was brought in and briefed on the situation to ensure law enforcement support for the extortion case and to assist with the eventual data leakage.

Although the ransom was never paid, there was a small amount of data leakage when the extortionist cashed in on a few records. But this development also helped the teams find more clues. The discovery of the records on the carder site provided a handle that was also used as a search term.

Ultimately, between the fraud team, IT support, and Earl's forensics team, a clearer picture and a subject started to come into focus. The final piece of the puzzle was one small cache file of a shadow internet session that was discovered in one of the images. It was the exact same file that was sent to the CEO in the original extortion letter. One file was the final nail.

With that small piece of evidence, Earl knew the name of the person who had possession of the device that had sent the extortion note. With the Secret Service leading a bank account analysis, the team found an unusual deposit on the same day that the stolen records showed up on the carder site.

The fraud and forensics teams did the last piece of the investigation: an onsite interrogation of the suspect, along with several other witness interviews.

By the end of a day of interrogations, Earl had all the evidence needed to close the case. The team contacted the Secret Service agent and explained all the evidence and witness accounts that had been gathered

Several weeks later, the Secret Service agent reported that the person had been arrested, taken to jail, and their brand-new car, which had been purchased with the ill-gotten funds, was impounded.

The power of forensics had never been so clear – and the value of a well-choreographed partnership between digital detective work and old fashion fraud hunting can never be overstated.

GREAT LEADERS FOSTER TEAMWORK – BUT HOW?

Every successful leader recognizes the immense importance of their team. There are many aspects to achieving business success, but there is near consensus within the technology and cybersecurity industries that organizations will succeed or fail based on their level of teamwork.

One way to demonstrate this reality is by looking at the words of top government and business leaders as they describe their career accomplishments.

James Collins, the exceptional Delaware Chief Information Officer (CIO) who was also the president of the National Association of State CIOs (NASCIO), said of his greatest successes, "In general, public servants don't get the credit they deserve. But I have had the honor of working with some of the most talented, dedicated, and conscientious people anywhere. We've been able to build relationships that have resulted in achieving positive and meaningful outcomes for Delawareans, businesses and visitors. . . ."[1]

When Phil Bertolini, the outstanding CIO from Oakland County, Michigan, left government service after a career of setting the global standard for technology leadership in local governments, he said this about his team: "Most of all, I will remember the incredible people that I worked with for 31 years. They were always there to ensure that our services were the best they could be. . . ."[2]

When Earl Duby, now CISO of Lear Corporation, says what sets apart Lear from other enterprises, he starts with the security culture – and how that comes through teamwork. "Building a culture of security is not just about providing informational resources to employees. More importantly, our strategy hinges on genuine *engagement* of our people. We've modified the conventional corporate training model going beyond the normal posters and email approach to awareness. We 'market' InfoSec best practices as a matter of personal importance that promotes the protection of home and family, not just Lear. Incentivized learning, gamified training modules, podcasts, animations, on-site events, and activities are combined with innovative thinking to create a diverse and multi-channeled learning environment. . . ."[3]

During his tenure as Missouri Government's Chief Information Security Officer, Mike Roling gained a national reputation for excellence and innovation. He attributes his success to his team and their teamwork: "[My] top memories involved working closely with my team and my peers under difficult situations. Multiple times during my tenure as CISO, state government was under siege by various threat actors. While these were strenuous times, strong teamwork combined with a little grit and ingenuity got us through them."[4]

SEVEN TIPS TO IMPROVE TEAMWORK

So how do we get there? What makes a great team – and how can you foster more effective teamwork? Here are seven tips to consider for cybersecurity and technology teams:

1. Build and retain the right team. Surround yourself with excellent people who not only have the right skills and know the business, but share your values and passion for excellence and results.

> ## TIP
>
> *There are lots of books and articles about making sure you have the right people on the bus before you get going.* Jim Collins, who wrote Good to Great, *has written an article closely examining building a team.[5] He starts with a long list of myths regarding change and success. From stock options to fear to acquisitions, these myths are "wrong, wrong, wrong." The correct answer starts with the people on the team.*

2. Take care of your staff. Once the right team is in place, take care of them. Reward accomplishments. This can be difficult in many organizations – especially on government teams. Take personal responsibility to use every tool available to help your team members achieve professional success. This includes doing the necessary paperwork for promotions, bonuses, and more. Celebrate personal accomplishments while recognizing professional achievements.

> ## TIP
>
> *Celebrate professional successes of team members – as a team. This means highlighting certifications, promotions or other key career milestones.*

3. Start planning with a blank sheet of paper (again). Take some time to clear the schedule and think about what projects truly need to be done by your group and why – starting from nothing. In accounting, this approach is called zero-based budgeting.[6] It may even help free up time and allow you to stop doing some tasks this year. Going through this exercise with your direct reports helps bring about ownership and support for others on the team.

> **TIP**
>
> *If a blank sheet is too hard, consider challenging your team to take three tasks off and add two for the coming reporting period.*

4. Lead by example. Great teamwork starts with effective team leaders who are fair, confident, kind, professional, and accessible. Every team leader can get to know their team members in a personal way and challenge them to contribute in meaningful, measurable ways.

By modeling consistent communication, including in-person and virtual (multi-channel) messages that are clear and hold others accountable, team leaders demonstrate group dynamic expectations.

> **TIP**
>
> *Look for a mentor in the industry you admire who is outside your immediate organization. Also, offer to give back and mentor others.*

5. **Get feedback.** Don't assume – measure how things are going on a regular basis.

How is the team performing? How do you know? One way is to ask team members, customers/clients, partners, and others who interact. Don't just rely on the experienced professionals – the perspective of new team members is also important.

Remember that changing work situations can radically alter team chemistry and performance. For example, the COVID-19 pandemic made working from home the new norm for most teams. When team interactions are 100% virtual, morale and teamwork can suffer, even if short-term productivity measurements remain high.

> **TIP**
>
> *Ask team members to propose practical ways to support each other and improve communication and morale in your particular team situation. Consider both virtual and in-person actions. Include process and technology solutions in recommended changes.*

6. **Expect (and plan for) the unexpected.** Ask the team: What could go wrong? Are we ready if it does? In the technology and security world, bad news (such as outages or data breaches or other emergencies) can define your legacy if you are not careful, so make sure you are prepared for the worst. You will have unexpected incidents; plan for them now.

> **TIP**
>
> *In nontechnical areas, check to ensure that your business continuity plans (BCP) are up to date for various emergency scenarios. Practice together with emergency management exercises – such as a tabletop exercise.*

7. Have fun – celebrate team success. There is a tendency to assume that security is never "done," which in one sense is true. However, you can celebrate key milestones and deliverables, recognize accomplishments and take time to document and show off best practices and awards. This will help build team pride in a job well done and foster team unity.

> **TIP**
>
> *Pick local sports events (such as March Madness basketball viewing of local teams), birthdays, picnics, or pot lucks for any reason. Have people come wearing their favorite team colors.*

CHAPTER 8

What Went Right?

Mistakes are a fact of life. It is the response to the error that counts.

–Nikki Giovanni

Bad news travels faster than good news. It is far easier to list everything a company has done wrong in a breach or an unexpected cyberattack. However, there is merit to studying what a company has done right. As we go through history and current affairs and the tales of the CISOs who have shared their stories with us, it's important to highlight the positives and identify important lessons from them. What did an American bank holding company do right? What can we learn from the aftermath of a hack on a renowned security vendor? What does the world's very first CISO have to say about today's times?

Most breaches are due to a variety of factors, from incorrect configuration to back door and application vulnerabilities, forgotten permissions, user errors, malware, insider threats, and the list goes on. In Capital One Financial Corporation's case, the firewalls were not properly configured, and their back door was left open – which is how the criminal got in, the same way she got into 30 other companies, as discovered by the FBI.

What was lost in translation in the frenzy of media coverage was Capital One's exceptional incident response. Many found the response of their then CISO, Michael Johnson, and his team impressive. First and foremost, they acted fast.

SWIFTNESS MATTERS

The Capital One cybersecurity team detected the incident within a few days. That's crucial, as it's common for an adversary to be in the system for months before being detected.

Once detected, the team collected all logs and started the forensics on them. Additionally, law enforcement was notified, and joined the effort. As a result, the criminal was identified by Capital One, and the FBI made the arrest with the discovered evidence.

The time of detection to the time of arrest was 10 days, before the stolen information could be commoditized. There is even a video on YouTube of reporters accompanying law enforcement to the apprehension. The whole experience served as a deterrent for other cyber criminals and bolstered public confidence in the capabilities of law enforcement.

At the same time, Capital One leadership promptly alerted the public of the cyber event, and they kept their communications transparent and authentic. CEO Richard Fairbank acted fast and told the public what they had detected, that law enforcement was notified immediately, and how they had the upper hand on the criminal. He also shared the necessary steps taken to ensure that it would not happen again, and that the data was not compromised beyond the criminal. In a statement, Fairbank said, "I am deeply sorry for what has happened. I sincerely apologize for the understandable worry this incident must be causing those affected and I am committed to making it right." The messaging was good, and it was sincere. Capital One acknowledged their mistakes, but it's also important to recognize what they got right and what, collectively, others can learn from their experience. First and foremost, they were able to detect the breach so quickly because they logged everything.

Retaining logs has long been a requirement in the U.S. government. There can be more than 14 years' worth of logs available to analyze in the event of a cyber event.[1] In contrast, there are still a lot of organizations in the private sector that do not retain their logs; many purge or rewrite them after 30 days. As such, the loss of data means that a tremendous amount of forensic ability is also lost. Without the logs, it is virtually impossible to identify malicious actors.

Ideally, you would want to keep your data for up to six months or a year. However, if you are facing campaign actions, it would be logical to keep at least more than a year's worth of data so that proper forensics can be done. It really depends on the risk exposure of your business in the event of a cyber attack.

Take the military environment as an example; they could afford to keep their data logs as storage has become increasingly inexpensive and more elastic. Every organization needs to make their own decision.

Finally, the importance of an incident response plan cannot be overstated. Every business should have one, and it should be constantly fine-tuned.

PROACTIVE LEADERSHIP AND TRANSPARENCY AS KEY FACTORS

In Shamane's blackout series, one of her CISO sessions happened to fall on the day after the aftermath and hack on FireEye, one of the largest cybersecurity vendors in the United States. Much of the session highlighted what the CTO did right: he deliberately went through the checklist of what to do in the event of a breach and in his public statement, he owned the problem and did not make excuses: "This is what happened, this is what we know about this, we are going to share with everyone, our experience is hopefully going to help others prepare and prevent against similar attacks."

Proactive leadership can aid in preserving the brand of the business in critical times such as a cyberattack and help keep stock prices from plunging.

The 2020 SolarWinds breach had a lot of collateral damage as it was a supply chain attack and many companies, including Microsoft, Cisco, and FireEye, were affected in different ways. Even now, when security professionals are asked to give an example of an organization that did well during a cyber crisis, FireEye is highlighted in a positive light.

In Singapore, Leong Boon explained why he believes they are a great industry example: "FireEye handled the incident very well. They were the first to be hit and the first to announce that they'd been breached, even before the SolarWinds attack came about, which turned out to be the root cause of their breach."

From the onset when the incident was discovered and announced, the tools that were stolen as a result of the breach were immediately released as open-source tools. This enabled FireEye's users, and even non-FireEye customers, to have a plan around their remediation efforts if required. FireEye went on to do very effective IR, which discovered the third-party breach in SolarWinds, which then led to many other discoveries along the way. The speed and transparency at which they announced their findings along the entire investigation was admirable.

FireEye, being an IR company that deals with large-scale investigations all the time, could have kept the information to themselves and their customers, choosing to reveal the bare minimum. However, all their reports were comprehensive. This allowed other organizations around the world to do what was necessary to detect whether they were one of the victims as well.

At the end of the day, cybersecurity is about a community effort rather than an individual's. Globally, we are all fighting the same war. The threat actors have infinite resources whether they are cyber syndicates or nation-state sponsored. If we do not bend together, they will defeat us. Ultimately, cybersecurity is about human versus human, not human versus machine. With that, there is going to be a continual evolution of the "Police vs Thief" game we are so familiar with; therefore, we all need to gather to fight the common enemy."

AVIATION INDUSTRY LESSONS FROM A CRISIS COMMUNICATIONS RESEARCHER

As a former media planner in Singapore's Ministry of Defence (MINDEF) and one of the writers of the MINDEF's crisis communications handbook, crisis communications researcher Kevin Kok-Yew Tan shared his thoughts about the timeliness of crisis response based on the severity of the crisis.

In crisis communication, the severity and crisis attribution (apportion of blame) decides how an organization should respond. In MINDEF, accidents and deaths and some of the conventional crises they prepare for, and the scale of severity, differ across different industries and types of organization.

One of the crises Kevin handled was the formation of the Haze Inter-Ministerial Committee (HIMC) in 2013, which dealt with one of the worst haze crises in Singapore. As MINDEF was the lead ministry, Kevin was part of the team that led the whole-of-government communications, including issuing press releases twice a day for the daily updates, managing ministerial visits, doorstop interviews, and international press conferences for the HIMC. This was good preparation for something less pleasant in 2014, when Malaysian Airlines MH370 went missing – one of aviation's greatest mysteries to date.

Kevin was the lead media planner for MINDEF, while the search was on in the Gulf of Thailand. While sending out press updates and managing the deluge of media requests and queries coming in due to their responsiveness and search capabilities, he and his team flew with the media on military aircraft in search of MH370, and planned support missions by air and sea for weeks.

The magnitude of an air crash would need some of the most experienced crisis communicators, many of whom are in the airline industry and airport operations. There is much to be learned from them for other industries.

The CONSOLE framework is one of the earliest crisis communication frameworks authored by Kevin together with Augustine Pang and Janelle Xiaoting Kang.[2] This framework puts together what crisis communicators in the aviation industry have to go through, similar to a doctor or nurse breaking bad news.

- Coherence: Need to be consistent; repetition of core messages.
- Orientation: Need to understand the audience; anticipate stakeholders' concerns and questions, and tailor communication to meet their informational needs.
- Nuance: Need to provide easy-to-understand technical information; use simple and unambiguous words and language or explanation of technical terms.
- Support: Mention support team/channels.
- Ongoing: Communication is ongoing, two-way engagement. Provide a way to give stakeholders the opportunity to address their concerns and questions.
- Leadership: The organization takes the lead to show the way ahead and the options available to the stakeholders.
- Empathy: Communicate messages that are high in emotional support and exhibit sensitivity.

While information is not always available, acknowledging the crisis and providing a channel for updates provides an official and verified source of information rather than letting online discussions or rumors perpetuate. In academia, an "information vacuum" and "stealing the thunder" are some of the areas crisis communication scholars have spent years researching. The current communication landscape no longer allows silence during crises. With opportunists in the misinformation space, whether satirical or not, losing its voice in a crisis can be detrimental to an organization's reputation.

Acknowledging a crisis or breach, establishing a dark site, announcing official channels for updates, and seeding third parties as advocates to offer an alternate voice (speaking for your organization) are processes that can and should be established before a crisis.

Some recommended strategies for organizations are regular simulation exercises to test the crisis communication processes, red-teaming communication processes, and developing scenario or situational flowcharts.

Providing an international perspective to crisis communication, Kevin concludes, "The internet and social media have closed the communication gaps globally, and we are left with cultural context which we should continue to nuance and pay attention to. While communicating in a crisis, the worst would be to blow up the crisis further due to the wrong cultural context, which fuels trolls and opportunists who might fan the flame. Conventionally, racial and religious sensitivities in Southeast Asia seem to affect the audience more than political sensitivities in other parts of the world. As digital communication continues to thrive, we are seeing less of such divides globally."

COMMUNICATING CYBER CRISIS WITH CONSOLE

- Let's break down how companies can apply **CONSOLE** in their communication. Always state the incident clearly. Be specific and consistent. Ambiguity results in seeds of doubts and uncertainty; always refer to past communication and stay coherent with the message(s) communicated.

   Company X would like to provide an update regarding the status of the data breach of XYZ records (containing names, birthdates, and addresses) that were found to be publicly accessible on a web server managed by a third-party provider.

- Always state the cause of the cyber crisis and address possible information gaps. Do not downplay the seriousness of the incident or the risk of access and misuse, and avoid leaving information vacuums for others to fill. Show your customers that you care about their personal information and concerns as much as they do.

This was due to a human error of an employee of the third-party vendor, and we will provide more updates as we progress in our investigations.

- Demonstrate **Empathy**.

Company X is deeply regretful to have caused any concerns with their customers as having their customers' trust is of great importance.

Here are some good examples of empathetic statements by CEOs of organizations:

"This is a very disappointing event for our company and strikes at the heart of who we are and what we do. I apologize to our customers for causing concern and frustration. We are conducting a thorough review of our overall security operations. We are also focused on customer protection and have developed a comprehensive service to support everyone, regardless of whether they were impacted by this incident." – Chairman and CEO of Equifax[3]

"None of this should have happened, and I will not make excuses for it. While I can't erase the past, I can commit on behalf of every Uber employee that we will learn from our mistakes. We are changing the way we do business, putting integrity at the core of every decision we make and working hard to earn the trust of our customers." – CEO of Uber[4]

- State actions taken to remediate.

Upon being notified, Company X took the below immediate steps to contain the breach and notified affected individuals.

Some examples include:

- Informed the Office of the Information Commissioner.
- Confirmed that any copies of the externally leaked data files were deleted.
- Engaged an independent security partner to do a risk assessment of the personal information compromised and forensic analysis on the exposed server.

- Brought in external experts to review existing processes extending to assessments of third parties.
- Monitored the dark web for any indication that the data was available or was being traded.
- Demonstrate **Leadership**.

  Company X has established a dedicated website that customers can visit if there are additional questions, or call a dedicated call center/toll-free number for direct assistance.
- Offer and show **S**upport.

  Company X will continue to exert great effort in providing assistance on the ongoing investigation. Company X remains committed to achieving the best outcome for its customers and will take all reasonable steps necessary to achieve this.
- State actions or changes that will be taken moving forward to prevent future occurrences.

Through all of this, **N**uance has been taken into consideration, ensuring easy-to-understand technical information. There is **C**oherence and consistency in the message, and the audience reaction has been preempted and catered to (**O**rientation). Finally, **O**ngoing communication needs to continually happen. Look at a variety of different platforms in reaching out to the affected individuals; overnotification is not an issue. Quite the contrary, individuals appreciate receiving direct and comprehensive communication.

MEET THE WORLD'S FIRST CISO

Steve Katz shared a story that was foundational to his becoming the world's first CISO. "When I first took the job in 1994, Citigroup (then Citicorp) was hacked by a group in Russia. I was told two things when I got the job: build the best information security organization around the world and they would give me a blank check to do it. There was already a rumor on Wall Street that Citigroup was hacked, and they confirmed it privately with me before I took the job."

Citigroup was planning to announce the hack a month after Steve started. In those four weeks, they wanted him to meet with their top 20 international clients and help ensure that they did not lose them. Steve continued, explaining, "But what motivated me to take up the challenge was the blank check they offered to build them the best cybersecurity program in the world."

Steve shared how he did this:

First, he established new policies, a single page of security principles, and a page for each principle – all in plain, simple English.

He then put in an ethical hacking program (remember, this was way back in the 1990s).

Steve also made sure that everyone he hired on the team was smarter than he was and knew more than he did. *Steve built a well-coordinated team.*

Steve explained: "My job was to be a visionary leader, and my team's job was to make it happen. If something does go wrong, I take the blame, and if something goes well, my team takes the credit. If you're not going to be a secure leader, don't lead."

Once Steve organized his solution, he set up global meetings with the heads of trade, CFOs, and other relevant stakeholders. "I put myself in the shoes of the CFOs; what are they concerned about? Is the CIA (confidentiality, integrity, availability) of the information important? Regarding a transaction, would they want a signed receipt? If there is a problem, would they want to know about it and how soon? If the problem results in technology being down, what would be an acceptable time for the systems to be back online again?"

Steve then prepared his response accordingly: "Here's my answer now; here's how we are doing it today, and here's how we will answer it in a year's time." He outlined the list of improvements they would work on and its timeline.

Steve also asked Citigroup's top 20 customers to take this list to the security teams in their own companies and see how they answered these same questions in their own companies. Then he told these executives to also take the questions to the other banks they were dealing with and compare the answers.

Interestingly, every single one of them came back with the same answer. They were not able to get visibility: the other banks did not want to discuss the questions about security, as it gave them exposure.

Steve also gave them his personal home and pager numbers and told them that if they had a security problem, they could find him. He strongly believed that when you make things simple and understandable, people will want to work with you.

Citigroup's upfront approach, with its proactive and transparent communication, reassured their customers and instilled confidence in the team, as compared to the lack of transparency with security by the other banks.

THE BASIC KEYS OF DISASTER RESPONSE

Former Scotland Yard Assistant Commissioner John Yates shared his general industry observation. "Companies who suffer a cyberattack resulting in a loss of personal data or privacy compromise, the ones who generally come out stronger, are those who acknowledge an incident has happened, respond and communicate swiftly, address privacy concerns and its impact well, and often come out of it with their reputation unharmed."

Now the director of security at Scentre Group, a Living Centre enterprise operating under the Westfield brand across Australia and New Zealand, John recounts an example of a company in Australia that responded very well in the event of an incident. This happened in 2015 in what was described then as Australia's largest security breach, where the personal data of more than half a million blood donors, including information about "at-risk sexual behavior," were leaked from the Australian Red Cross Blood Service.

John expounded: "Oh, it's a horror story, but actually if you look at what they did as an organization, they had a plan, they communicated that plan effectively, that plan was exercised well, and there was absolute transparency. They did all those things extremely well and people within the industry can certainly say they came out of it with their reputation enhanced.

"The thing with cyberattacks that are so different from other forms of attacks is that you actually think you've got more time than you have. There is a tendency for senior executives, quite understandably I might add, to want to know 'everything' about a problem before deciding how to act. If you have lost customers' personal data, then any delay in telling them is unacceptable. This is a change in mindset that is tough for some senior people to deal with.

"There are also companies who go into denial – *this isn't happening to us*. It either doesn't get escalated quickly enough, or their response plans haven't been well thought through or exercised. They are furtive, reluctant to disclose or contact the victims, or they do it very slowly. That is cataclysmic for a company's reputation.

"What I've learned through my past policing is that the environment now is so much focused on people and victims that you ignore that at your peril. It's a victim-centered approach, and understanding its impact is critically important, not just from an emotionally intelligent perspective, but just managing and thinking through the consequences and considering what happens to the company's reputation.

"We used to have a saying in policing, following any badly managed crisis: 'RIP' which isn't 'Rest in Peace' but 'Reputation in Pieces.' It's literally that."

The Australian Red Cross Blood Service accepted full responsibility for the incident and did well in their response:[5]

- They continued to engage with the Incident Management Service of AusCERT by telephone and in person to assist its response to the incident.

- They confirmed that a copy of the data file that was leaked externally had been deleted.
- They engaged an identity and cyber support service to undertake an independent risk assessment of the personal information compromised.
- They issued press releases confirming that a data breach had occurred and published statements on their website and social media sites.
- They established a dedicated website, telephone hotline, and email inquiry facility to respond to public inquiries.
- They notified affected individuals via text message or email.
- They engaged specialist organizations to conduct forensic analysis on the exposed precedent server, monitor their website for any vulnerabilities or unusual activity, and monitor the dark web for any indication that the data was available or was being traded.

In summary, these very basic key things – having a plan, exercising that plan in a timely manner, executing perfect communication, and having a victim-centered approach – reduce the likelihood of adverse consequences for affected individuals.

This works for our world of cybersecurity as it works for any disaster.

THE PROBLEM WITH MISINFORMATION

Although it may seem obvious, the single most important thing a leader in a crisis needs to have is absolute clarity about what has happened. Your source is clear, and you have intelligence that is understood; John Yates refers to the 5x5x5 intelligence, the National Intelligence Model in use in the UK and adopted elsewhere,[6] which provides an indication of the level of confidence that can be held in valuing any particular piece of intelligence or information. (See Figure 8.1.) This informs decision making and supports interoperability between agencies/organizations.

Source and Information/Intelligence evaluation to be completed by submitting officer

	A	B	C	D	E
Source evaluation	Always reliable ☐	Mostly reliable ☐	Sometimes reliable ☐	Unreliable ☐	Untested source ☐
	1	2	3	4	5
Information/ intelligence evaluation	Known to be true without reservation ☐	Known personally to the source but not to the person reporting ☐	Not known personally to the source but corroborated ☐	Cannot be judged ☐	Suspected to be false ☐
Intelligence unit only	1	2	3	4	5
Handling code To be completed by the evaluator on receipt and prior to entry onto the intelligence system	**Default: Permits** dissemination within the UK police service **and** to other law enforcement agencies as specified.	Permits dissemination to UK nonprosecuting parties. [Conditions apply]	Permits dissemination to (non-EU) foreign law enforcement agencies. [Conditions apply]	Permits dissemination within originating service/agency only; specify reasons and internal recipient(s). Review period must be set.	Permits dissemination but receiving agency to observe conditions as specified.
To be reviewed on dissemination	☐	☐	☐	☐	☐

FIGURE 8.1 5x5x5 National Intelligence Model

"You need to have the very best picture of what has happened," John said. "For so many crises (physical/cyber/any sort), the response becomes distorted because people aren't clear about what has happened. In the security services and government world I used to inhabit, the national crisis management committee in the UK called the Cabinet Office Briefing Room A (COBRA) would first start any crisis management meeting room with the Commonly Recognized Information Picture (CRIP)."

CRIP typically consists of:

- Brief and accurate situation reports containing information relating to the incident
- Information on any significant wider impact
- Main developments and decisions
- Trends and upcoming decision points
- Scale of recovery issues and effectiveness of the response (using the agreed recovery reporting framework and principles)

CRIP would be summarized on display boards in COBRA and briefed at the outset of key meetings and shared as far as possible with responders at the regional and local level.

John further explains its mechanics: "The first thing they would start any crisis management meeting with was with CRIP, which will be provided normally by the home security services (if it's a domestic crisis), and foreign intelligence services (if it's a foreign crisis).

"CRIP helps to bring all the parties to a common understanding of what is known, and, more importantly, what is not known. That intelligence picture is the single most important thing for an executive/leader to understand, and not have the biased input about what the television/social media/rumour is saying. You need to absolutely understand what value you can put on the information being told."

John tells of the infamous 2017 Las Vegas Strip mass shooting, where 60 people died. Social media suggested there were multiple shootings taking place all over the city, which completely distorted the picture. "I've seen the presentation done by the police officer who was in charge. There was only one shooter in that hotel, but there were multiple reports – at least 10 separate mass shooting incidents that happened that people were responding to."

A cyber crisis is another vector that will create a lot of social media chatter. You will hear many different things, and get huge peripheral, sometimes inaccurate, and often exaggerated chatter. You've got to be very careful not to overreact, and of course not to underreact, saying it's just noise, as sometimes it might not be noise.

It is important for any leader or member of the advisory management team to have a common understanding. John continued, "You do not want someone to be having a separate briefing about one aspect and someone else having another briefing from elsewhere about a different aspect. Everyone needs to have a common understanding. It sounds fairly obvious but so many times I've seen people in crisis who either haven't listened, they've made assumptions, or they've indulged in groupthink."

John draws attention to something said by U.S. general George S. Patton: "If everyone is thinking alike, then somebody isn't thinking." John concluded, "You've got to really guard against that. Don't make assumptions. Have sound, intelligent advice and make a record of what you're doing."

THE STOCKWELL TUBE INCIDENT

In another example of misinformation, John recalled a case where a Brazilian electrician, Jean Charles de Menezes, was mistaken for a terrorist and shot dead by officers from the Metropolitan Police in London at the Stockwell Tube Station. They thought he was a suicide bomber.

The Commissioner went on television an hour or two afterwards and said, "The information I have available is that this shooting is directly linked to the ongoing and expanding anti-terrorist operation. Any death is deeply regrettable; I understand the man was challenged and refused to obey."

However, he gave this statement following an interview that had been broadcast on Sky News with a supposed eyewitness who said that he had seen what he had assumed to be the terrorist dressed in a bulky jacket, leaping barriers and running down the tube station. In fact, what the eyewitness saw was an armed police officer who was wearing the bulky jacket, jumping barriers, in pursuit of the "terrorist."

De Menezes, however, had not been running from the police. He did not vault over barriers; he was not even wearing a padded jacket that could have concealed a bomb. Instead he wore a denim jacket that hid nothing.[7]

The fact that the Commissioner, as the most senior police officer in the country, provided a misleading account of what had happened resulted in significant consequences on the trust and confidence the public had in his organization and the Metropolitan Police. The Commissioner eventually was forced to resign after this and numerous other missteps. Stockwell was always seen as the starting point of his descent.

Two weeks earlier, London had been attacked by a group of suicide bombers who killed 53 people and injured hundreds.[8] In the midst of this crisis situation, which was already a source of intense stress and pressure, the misdirection in briefings, poor incident planning, poor surveillance, and ambiguous instructions were among the many failings.

Effective intelligence, documentation, communication, and leadership are the hallmarks to any response to a cyberattack. John Yates further breaks down the four important keys:

1. Intelligence: It is important to collect intelligence to build up a detailed knowledge of the present or potential threats, assess, and investigate before deciding on the response and protective measures to take.
2. Record keeping: How do you keep your records and document incidents and actions for the future? Most crises either result in shareholder value going south, loss of life, or public inquiries, just to name a few, so you need to have absolute understanding of who is doing the documentation and what is being documented. As a very wise former senior officer once said, "If it isn't written down, it didn't happen."
3. Clarity of communication: Different sentences with different emphases mean different things to different people. When British Prime Minister Tony Blair went to Parliament and said that Iraq could deploy weapons of mass destruction within 45 minutes of an order and the threat is "imminent," what does that mean? Imminent could mean the next five minutes or the next four weeks – who knows? The onus is on the leader to be clear in their communication and make sure that people have the ability to seek

understanding, clarification, and confirmation of exactly what they are being told.

4. Leadership behavior: Do you create an environment with your team that invites challenge, response, criticism, and scrutiny, or do you have the mentality that just because you are a leader, no one is going to challenge you?

If you see a figure of authority, for example, a police officer, just because they have the crowns on their shoulder, the stars, and the hat does not mean that they are always right. Do you create an environment that invites purposeful challenges?

The Day After: Recovering from Cyber Emergencies

CHAPTER 9

The Road to Recovery

The ultimate measure of a man is not where he stands in the moments of comfort, but where he stands at times of challenge and controversy.

—Martin Luther King, Jr.

In a span of a month, Israel faced multi-pronged cyber incidents across the engineering, food, and education sectors. The Israeli cyber headquarters detected that hackers had triggered a vulnerability that was installed in a number of Israeli engineering subsidiaries across different countries. They were stealing sensitive information and sending it to an external IP address every week.

Additionally, a large food factory discovered a vulnerability that compromised their external services and could cause a toxic substance leak in the event of an incident. Finally, a huge academic center's server was shut down by a hacker who exploited a known vulnerability in a VPN product, and gained access to the organization.

CYBER MINDSETS FROM A WAR ZONE

Doron Sivan is one of the founders and the board chairman of the Israeli high-tech industry MadSec, a leading cybersecurity consulting company. He is the former CEO of Cronus Cyber Technologies.

Doron highlights those three cyber incidents and the work needed to tighten their defenses in the space of a short few weeks. He emphasizes that, for any chance of a healthy recovery, having a proactive mindset is important.

Doron shared those experiences while missiles were fired overhead in a span of two weeks, as happened in May 2021. MadSec usually sees an increase of DDoS attacks and attempts to corrupt websites and DNS during such times. "Luckily we are used to it, everyone worked regularly from home (with the kids) and from the shelters. These moments only reinforce the sense that everyone must always remain on high alert."

He explained that in Israel, unfortunately, simultaneous crises are quite common and offered his current situation as a live example. Despite this, MadSec continued work as usual.

The cyber headquarters provide initial support to affected customers and share updates on vulnerabilities found, including where customers' information has been posted and sold online. MadSec also directs customers to private companies in the field.

In Israel, the CISOs and their vendors use WhatsApp and Telegram groups to stay in close communication with one another. Any problems or suspicions are immediately flagged and get the most attention. Concerns are immediately brought to the attention of the Israeli government.

"Having a business continuity plan is very common here. There is no choice, given the fact that we are involved in war every five to six years, and when there is a country like Iran that clearly states that its goal is to destroy Israel. Having a BCP helps a lot during the pandemic times, and thus it also made sense in adding a chapter in business continuity for cyber events. This readiness helps in dealing with such incidents," Doron explains.

MadSec usually divides a cyber crisis into two waves. The first wave is more technological in nature and focuses on information recovery, forensics, negotiations with the attackers, and returning to normal business activities. The role of the first wave is to bring the organization back into operation.

A big part of the threat is what Doron calls the second wave, which deals with financial, legal, and public image aspects. This wave focuses on the fear of security customers' transactions being canceled (a significant issue in the Israeli market) and exposure to lawsuits related to privacy protection (the European market is very strict about their Privacy Protection Act, and companies in Israel carry out a lot of business activity in Europe).

A company's poor cyber health or awareness is perceived detrimentally in Israel. A company's reputation will be significantly damaged in the professional evaluation of the employees and by its customers. For a public company, its shares will be affected.

Doron concludes that while CISOs focus on dealing with the first wave, management is primarily concerned with the second wave, and sometimes, it is precisely this fear of the second wave that drives management to become more cyber aware today.

In any road to recovery, the basics are in ensuring that fixes are administered in a prompt manner. At the same time, it is important to be aware of other potential hindrances that you will have to navigate on this journey.

HINDRANCES TO AVOID

Theo Nassiokas (introduced in Chapter 4), currently an Australian-based cyber security and tech risk leader with a two-decade career in global financial services organizations, shares his observations of obstacles to avoid when on your recovery mission:

- Senior executives can get in the way of the response, containment, and resolution effort by insisting on constant reporting of updates regarding the attack. This diverts cyber leadership away from responding to the attack, thereby jeopardizing the response effort.

- Responses are often too IT-focused to the exclusion of legal, communications, and other critical departments, resulting in substandard responses to cyber attacks, particularly in high-profile, publicly reported events, leading to reputational damage.
- Third-party relationships are not properly security assessed, and instead are based on the financial relationship rather than on the risk posed by the supplier through data they're processing or storing on behalf of the business, such as personally identifiable information (PII).

In summary, companies need to be relatively open publicly about a cyberattack, their response to the attack, and any actual or potential loss suffered, including data compromise, systems failure, and network breach.

This should include learnings and next steps in response to the attack. Gaining or rebuilding consumer trust should be the focus. Customers must believe that a business is being honest about cyberattacks, and that they've responded appropriately and they'll improve through the experience. Customers lose confidence in any business appearing to cover up or downplay cyberattacks.

ASYMMETRIC HYBRID WARFARE (AHW)

At a more macro level, cyber security professionals must remain curious to understand the context in which cyberattacks exist. Cyber is a geopolitical issue; at a higher level it's an asymmetric warfare strategy. Cyberattacks are often a part of governments' foreign policies. The big picture is far larger than the actual technical cyberattack and its resulting impact.

In intelligence-led cyber, knowing "yourself" refers to understanding your people, process, and controls environment from a cybersecurity and cyber resilience controls perspective. Theo highlights the significance of the Stuxnet attack, the world's first digital weapon, first reported on in June 2010: "Stuxnet is significant because it it's one of the earliest well-publicized cases of Asymmetric Hybrid Warfare (AHW) allegedly used by national state actors to enact their foreign policy. As a result, many countries realized the value of using cyber-attacks as part of their AHW strategies."[1]

The Stuxnet attack was the brainchild of some of the best experts in the world.[2] Considered a first-of-its-kind virus, it was designed to stop or slow down Iran's nuclear program. This prolific cyberattack caused the first known destruction of critical infrastructure assets and revealed the power of cyber as a nation-state grade weapon. In doing so, cyberattacks were recognized as part of an AHW strategy as early as 2007, although likely were in use even earlier.

That is why, in the aftermath of any cyberattack, it is important for the board and executives to be attuned to the geopolitical affairs in the world. Stuxnet demonstrates that companies must be aware of and evaluate any changes in the foreign policy landscape and understand how and where their businesses fit in the bigger picture. This lens will help them plan their defenses better and understand how appropriate their investment will be.

THE ROAD TO NO RECOVERY

In the online Blackout Series – *Leadership in Crisis*, Brigadier General Gregory J. Touhill, former CISO for President Obama shares a 2015 incident with a third-party vendor working with the U.S. Office of Personnel Management (OPM).[3] A nation-state actor compromised the third party, which enabled the attacking group to break into the OPM system.

The hack started when an employee who had super system admin access posted on social media, which got the attention of the nation-state actor. The employee used the same username and password in several of his personal accounts. These were harvested in previous hacks of commercial enterprises that revealed his pattern of conduct.

The nation-state actors got into the network, elevated their privileges, moved laterally, and compromised everything within the third party within a couple of days. They were then able to get into the government system via its VPN as if they were a legitimate user.

This came to the attention of the Department of Homeland Security (DHS) in the middle of a counterespionage investigation. The organization reacted defensively and was in a state of denial. Instead of cooperating, they argued with DHS. They did not follow a crisis handbook nor did they have any process in place for what to do.

Instead, they put lawyers on the frontline, denied ownership, and refused to cooperate with the investigation. They even tampered with evidence and erased some logs in an attempt to cover up. This was foolish, especially when the majority of their business was government contracts.

Ultimately, the contracts were terminated, and the company went bankrupt within weeks of the attack. This was a sad example of an unprepared company that did not know how to react properly.

In the middle of a cyber breach, when the national CERTs are involved, it is crucial to cooperate. CERTs and law enforcement are also mindful that they would like to get you back up and running as soon as possible.

CISO leaders must recognize that information sharing is very important, not just with the investigators or law enforcement, but with information-sharing organizations. It should be part of building and contributing to the cybersecurity ecosystem. As cyber risk leaders, none of us are in it alone. In the United States, there is the Information Sharing Analysis Organization (ISAO), a cyber "neighborhood watch." The cybersecurity community is made better by sharing its experiences, learnings, and countermeasures. As President John F. Kennedy stated, "A rising tide lifts all boats."

THE FIRST STEP IN COMMUNICATION

After a cyber incident, the first step in addressing what went wrong and what needs to be worked on is understanding your audience. There are different forms of communication, and you must ensure that you are communicating well with the organization itself.

Always think of your audience and adapt your style accordingly. Within the organization, it is important to determine the types of communication leadership that are required to go down the different levels. However, communication is also required upwards, laterally, and externally.

From the start, driving the right engagement and leading first with recommendations are vital, before sharing key details to support your conclusion. Although it is helpful if there's some indication of the preferred type and style of information, it is important to consider the information that is most needed by the management without having to go into every detail. Think through the information that you need to push up and the best approach for it.

Communication with peers across departments is critically important; in addition, the message needs to be synchronized throughout the organization.

Finally, as highlighted in earlier chapters, consider the external communication to your customers, partners, and investors. Most businesses have third-party suppliers, business-to-business relationships, or board members who are sensitive to their current and prospective investors. Due care and due diligence are required in all communication to ensure that the right things are done in the right way at the right time.

THE FOUR STEPS OF A CRISIS-READY FORMULA

In the middle of a crisis recovery, a game plan needs to be prepared concurrently to avoid the same crisis again. It also is important that your staff are equipped in identifying the components that could contribute to the virality of a negative event. Usually, such events have a high emotional impact, and the more relatable to the general public and shareable the event is, the higher the chances that negative news is going to stick to your brand.

Cision Insights, a global provider of media software and services for PR and marketing communications professionals, compared two crisis responses, one from a technology company and one from a retail company. Upon encountering problems with their product, the retail company immediately recalled their product and issued an official statement. Of the company's spokespeople, 29% delivered the company's messages in the first week of the crisis. As a result, the negative news was balanced with a more active, extensive approach and controlled messaging coming from the brand itself.

The technology company took seven weeks before doing a product recall. They had far fewer spokespeople (8%) communicating the company's message and had to issue three different official statements as the negative media coverage continued. The retail company curbed their crisis phase to just two weeks as compared to nine weeks with the technology company.

Melissa Agnes, founder and CEO at Crisis Ready Institute, shares the Crisis Ready® Formula:[4]

1. *Be Thoughtful:* Seek to understand all sides and points of view of the controversy and its emotional relatability; think through the situation in alignment with the organization's core values; and assess all potential risks to the organization's reputation and its emotional connection with its stakeholders.
2. *Be Decisive:* Take a decisive stance in alignment with the organization's values. Because controversy segregates, know that you will not appeal to or please everyone, which means that being decisive is important. Don't make a decision you will go back on, and ensure that your team understands that some stakeholders will most likely not be happy.
3. *Be Clear:* Release a strong statement that clearly and concisely explains your position, decision, and reasoning. Do not be ambiguous or leave room for misinterpretation or misconception.

4. *Be Quiet and Monitor:* Once steps 1 through 3 have been taken, there is nothing left to say. Let the conversation take place, continue to monitor, and establish a threshold that, if surpassed, requires notification steps and escalation to leadership.

As we communicate down, up, across, and out, we need to factor in multiple audiences, and the timing and methodology of the messaging needs to be carefully crafted for each of them. Craft such messages ahead of time.

KEY ACTIONS FOR RECOVERY

Shaofei, CISO of Singapore's main transport sector, shared the following three key actions that are important for companies to recover well after a crisis.

The first step is *not to panic,* but to assemble the facts. Importantly, do not create additional tasks for the incident response team, such as documenting formal investigation reports, at this stage; leave them to execute the incident response playbook with affected stakeholders, which should include communication strategies. Again, this underscores the importance of developing and exercising incident response playbooks prior to any cyber emergency.

The next step is to understand the extent of the incident, and to contain the attack as far as practically possible. This task is more easily accomplished if organizations maintain a security architecture of their systems, including their operating system and software version details, and so on. Ideally, having a threat-hunting capability in the cybersecurity team is a strong value-add, as discovered artifacts and network traces could point to known attack TTPs (tactics, techniques, and procedures) employed by known threat actors; further containment measures could then focus on subsequent stages of cyber kill chains commonly used by those actors.

Last but not least, after-action reviews (AARs) and lessons learned from the cyber incident should be documented and archived in a knowledge management system, not merely as a process or procedure required by the regulator or similar agency but as a means of ensuring that the organization comes out stronger after each incident.

During a CISO forum, the panel was asked their view of a company that has suffered a major cyberattack. All were hesitant and opted to go with a competitor instead. The only way they would change their minds is if they had assurances from the breached company, a detailed understanding of lessons learned, what they were doing differently, and how they would respond differently the next time.

CHAPTER 10

What Went Wrong – How Did We Miss It?

You can't connect the dots looking forward; you can only connect them looking back-
wards. So you have to trust that the dots will somehow connect in your future. You
have to trust in something – your gut, destiny, life, karma, whatever. This approach
has never let me down, and it has made all the difference in my life.

—Steve Jobs[1]

The long lines of cars and trucks waiting for gasoline showed America
what failure looks like when it comes to protecting critical infrastructure from a cyberattack. Panic buying became rampant in southeastern U.S. states after the Colonial Pipeline was struck with DarkSide
ransomware in May 2021,[2] which forced the company to shut down
operations for several days.

As gas shortages struck Virginia, North Carolina, South Carolina,
Georgia, and other states, more Americans than ever before were given
a crash course in the definition of ransomware.

Sure, there had been many ransomware attacks against international companies, local businesses, and cities like Baltimore, Atlanta,
and Philadelphia. There had been previous headline-grabbing cyberattacks against hospitals – even causing the death of a woman in
Germany.[3] But somehow, none of those local, national, or global cybersecurity incidents grabbed national attention like the gas lines in the

Carolinas, perhaps because America was just starting to emerge the COVID-19 pandemic and was ready to focus on other things.

Instead, this ransomware incident became the global wake-up call and tipping point for wider cyber attention, and the immediate fallout was immense. In addition to President Biden's cabinet members making media appearances with clear talking points, a lengthy Executive Order on Cybersecurity was hurriedly released, with tight deadlines for federal action.[4]

At the same time, the U.S. defense and intelligence communities were busy hacking back. Not surprisingly, one week after the cyberattack, the hacker, DarkSide, announced it would shut down operations.[5] But most cyber experts declared that DarkSide would likely just reappear within a few months under a new name.

What became painfully clear to the U.S. general public as well as global bad actors in the aftermath was that large sections of America's critical infrastructure were extremely vulnerable to cyberattacks[6] – and that the ransom demand was paid to the tune of $5 million. In this case, sadly, cybercrime did pay. *Note: The FBI was able to recover approximately $2.3 million in Bitcoin after the incident.*

Those who took the extra time to look even deeper could now connect the dots. They saw the many other ransomware and other cyber incidents (before and after the gas lines). They now realized we were in the midst of a (global) ransomware crisis.

In a harsh sense, the troubling Colonial Pipeline cyber incident did the international community a favor. It unmasked America's, and the world's, ongoing cyber emergency situation without the devastation of a 9/11 or cyber Pearl Harbor event.

The question is, will society too soon forget?

MISTAKES AND SOLUTIONS IN WISCONSIN

Bill Nash, the former CISO for the state of Wisconsin, recently looked back at their cyber journey, and he saw the good, the bad, and the ugly.

"While what we have for partnerships and cyber response in Wisconsin today is amazing, I must say that we were not perfect out of the gate and did not really understand what we were doing. In reality, it has been more of a build-the-plane-as-you-fly-it adventure.

"When we first started planning the CRT capability, we thought we needed to prepare 10 member teams with specific cybersecurity skills to defend against and respond to major cyberattacks on critical infrastructure conducted by nation-state actors. Well, as it turns out, the real need was much more basic than that.

"One ransomware incident we responded to presented us with a situation where the backup server had been encrypted and even though the backup media was not encrypted, they could not be restored without the server. The organization's person who knew that software was out of state and not available. Fortunately, we had a CRT team member who knew this specific backup software and he drove two hours to help.

"Today, we not only track the cyber classes/certifications our team members have, but we also track what IT products they know and can support. When assembling the team to respond, we don't assume it is made up of individuals from a 10-member team in a regional area; it is based on skills needed and who is able to volunteer.

"We also learned that many activities, like sifting through log data, packet captures, and malware scripts, can be done remotely. We just need the on-site team to do the forensic collection and put the pieces in place to get the recovery rolling. It seems so simple when we think about it six years later."

Building working relationships with Wisconsin's federal partners turned out to be tricky as well.

When the Illinois State Board of Elections website was hacked in 2016, compromising a voter registration database, it made national headlines. Their federal partners and the Multi-State Information Sharing and Analysis Center (MS-ISAC) did a great job of sharing the compromise indicators with Wisconsin and the other states.

As such, the Wisconsin team blocked the IP addresses, some of which had been blocked for other reasons, and reviewed the log information to look for traffic from those addresses. They discovered some scans that were blocked in a public job center.

They shared the logs and context of what was found with federal partners, but unfortunately as the information went up the chain it got misinterpreted that Wisconsin was one of multiple state election systems hacked by the Russians.

The team laughs about that situation now, but at the time it created a nightmare of press inquiries to deal with something that was an event log showing traffic dropped by the firewall.

Their local and federal leaders were unhappy, and many improvements were made to keep it from happening again. Wisconsin continues to share data with federal partners, and it is definitely a value-add.

One lesson they learned was that when you include National Guard members as part of the onsite response team, it is better if they go in civilian clothes. They learned this when responding to a K–12 incident, when the press received reports from parents that the school's systems were down and the military had been called in.

HOSPITAL RANSOMWARE – AND LEARNING FROM MISTAKES

Scott Larsen is an experienced, well-respected CISO who has led security teams at Beaumont Hospital in Michigan and Inova Healthcare in Virginia – in addition to being the co-founder of the Michigan Healthcare Cybersecurity Council (MiHCC). Scott shared these incident stories offering mistakes, lessons learned, and helpful advice.

"The most memorable cybersecurity incident that I have experienced was undoubtedly the Nuance incident of 2017. Nuance provides speech and imaging software to various industries including healthcare. In this case the healthcare organization with which I was employed used the electronic transcription services offered by Nuance that were implemented using cloud-based technology.

"This attack affected over 15,000 hospitals across the globe. In response to this NotPetya malware attack, Nuance pulled the plug on their servers to limit the damage and as a result made this transcription service unavailable to all of its customers from late July through August of 2017.

"The details and financial impact were revealed in the aftermath and proved to be substantial. For my organization, the impacts were evident in lost productivity and implementation of a manual process for transcription that took much longer. According to SEC 10-Q filings provided by Nuance, the company's losses in revenue approached $68 million, and remediation and recovery costs were estimated at approximately $24 million. These numbers do not, however, take into account the negative impact of the company's reputation. I'm fairly certain that today their security posture is far stronger, as they likely have increased their investment in their cybersecurity protections as a result of this incident.

"There are several key takeaways from this incident. One in particular was the importance of disaster recovery and business continuity plans and the exercise thereof. Our own program's focus on periodic tabletop exercises served us very well. It was also very evident that we should ensure that all our vendor partners have strong response plans that demonstrate a preparedness and resilience capability to protect and recover from these types of attacks. Every organization should focus on integrating this important factor into vendor management processes. This will serve to protect every healthcare organization's operational status as well as patient data.

"The importance of exercising incident response plans was also a major learning in this incident. Because our team had documented and exercised our incident response plan we were able to respond to this incident in an expert and effective manner. Most of you are familiar with the adage 'practice makes perfect.' I would suggest an alternate version of this adage 'practice makes permanent.' My team was well prepared and responded effectively to this crisis due to our focus on documenting our incident response plans and practicing them on a regular basis.

"We must continually strive to improve and strengthen our incident response processes by conducting periodic exercises that involve different levels of our respective organizations. A product of these exercises would include adjustment of our plans as we learn more about our own preparedness and the cyber threats that continue to evolve.

"Coordination efforts with external partner organizations were another important aspect of the successful response to this incident. I like to call this our 'Collaborative Advantage.' When we share best practices and freely share information about indicators of compromise in an environment of trust, it makes us all better and more secure. These relationships were something that I developed during my career and my tenure as a chief information security officer and cybersecurity leader.

"Our organization definitely benefited from our existing strong relationships with both law enforcement partners from the state and federal level as well as our healthcare brethren through our collective membership in the Michigan Healthcare Cybersecurity Council, Inc. The information sharing and collaboration advantage (with other hospitals and health systems) was essential in obtaining additional situational intelligence and vital information to inform decisions in real time."

HOW OVERCONFIDENCE CAN IMPACT ORGANIZATIONAL SECURITY AND CAUSE DATA BREACHES

Pride comes before a fall. This plays out in many areas of life, from sports upsets to defending business networks from data breaches.

Some believe that there are so many data breaches because the bad actors are just too good. The real answer may be a culture of IT pride and individual practices that are prevalent in many top-tier organizations, including top consulting firms, tech companies, and three-letter government agencies in Washington, D.C. and around the world.

Such a culture is not about striving for excellence, pride of skill or craft or profession, or being "proud of a job well done"; it is a blind spot type of pride that plays out as overconfidence and/or a lack of preparation and/or not "bringing your A-game" into a situation.

And yet, security professionals hear this message all the time: "It won't happen to us."

Three examples of this principle in real life include:

1. Equifax not patching a well-known vulnerability that led to a massive breach.[7]
2. Equifax using the word "admin" for the login and password of an important database with sensitive information.[8]
3. Deloitte's enterprise email administrators not using two-factor authentication, which resulted in a data breach.[9]

These three cases cannot be attributed to a lack of corporate resources nor to a lack of company expertise to fix these problems. In fact, both companies teach others how to do these things. The same issues of overconfidence could even be used in critical infrastructure protection by wealth companies – such as in the Colonial Pipeline incident.

Here are 10 ways that executive management, alongside technology and security pros, often fail under the banner of pride or overconfidence, possibly even leading to negligence:

1. Not putting the right person or the right team(s) on the right task(s), or assigning them properly initially but then pulling them off and bringing in the B- or C-team, or using student interns to run things at night or over weekends or during vacations to save money. Note: Top tech firms and consultants strive to place their best experts where they can be billed for the highest price.
2. Not fully implanting tools, processes, or procedures. Also, not enforcing policies, such as allowing enterprise email administrators to forego two-factor authentication, or not providing the training required. Note: This challenge can flow from professional

overconfidence when some think that they "wrote the book" and already know enough to break their own rules. As Morpheus said in the movie *The Matrix*, "There's a difference between knowing the path and walking the path."

3. Underestimating your adversary, while overestimating a technology tool's ability to stop incidents – perhaps even with junior staff; not preparing properly to implement new security and technology projects.

4. Highly qualified staff not bringing their A-game for any personal or professional reason.

5. Assuming that everything is being done right without checking, basing decisions on bad metrics, or feeling that enough is already being done, since millions of dollars have already been spent on cybersecurity.

6. Assuming that the outsourced function (by support vendor or their team) is taking care of things properly (overconfidence in vendor's ability), without understanding that you can't outsource the responsibility.

7. Staff not wanting to ask needed questions out of fear of reprisal and/or telling their management things that could get them disciplined. Staff can even give up after repeated warnings. Note: Overconfident management can also ignore warnings that they have heard from staff before because staff seem to be "crying wolf."

8. Not being willing to change with the times regarding security tools and techniques when cyberattacks change – "We've always done it this way."

9. Burned-out teams. Executives believe that since the team has performed incident response miracles in the past, they'll somehow do it again. But now the team is worn- out and ill- equipped to keep performing at a top level. Good management understands that cybersecurity incident response teams can only continue for so long without breaks or reinforcements.

10. Management's lack of understanding of what talent they really have. Yes, they were the best a few years back, but maybe their top cyber talent left. Some managers don't want the executives to know they are in trouble.

There are certainly times when top teams bring their A-game and still get beat by some nation-state or other hacker A-team. The best players and tools and processes and overall cyber defense can certainly be overmatched despite an organization's best efforts.

But that is not what happens in the vast majority of cyber incidents. Cyber criminals go after the easiest targets, and far too many organizations do the basic security tasks poorly.

Moving forward, executives must collectively look in the mirror and recognize that they can do better. With cyber best practices being followed, such as good patching, proper cyber hygiene, the basic cyber-blocking and tackling tasks, updated security awareness training for all staff, and implementing the Cyber Framework checklists from NIST or others, most data breaches can be avoided.

An important message to cybersecurity pros is this: Stay humble and vigilant. You never know what or who is around the next corner.

REFLECTING ON INCIDENTS WITH A MENTOR

One of the best ways to help your team improve and also to grow in your professional career is to reflect on key leadership events and major incidents with a mentor who has been through cybersecurity incident battles before. There are many ways to find a helpful mentor, and your sector coordinating council or other professional organization can help.

For example: "The goal for the MS-ISAC Mentoring Program is to provide an opportunity for security leaders in management positions (chief information security officers and chief security officers) to network and learn from the experience of current security leaders. These professional partnerships, through regular communication, were to foster a trusted mentor/mentee relationship. The opportunity provides the mentee with a valued partner for problem-solving, career guidance, and insight into shared experiences and solutions."[10]

There are CISO communities and forums to tap into for their top lessons. In research conducted by Shamane and published in her book *Cyber Risk Leaders: Global C-Suite Insights – Leadership & Influence in the Cyber Age*,[11] she interviewed multiple groups of CISOs across diverse sectors and countries. Their advice includes:

- Prepare to be wrong and do not be afraid to admit it.
- Accept being the bearer of bad news.
- Seek executive support; a supportive CEO makes all the difference to the success of the CISO.
- Be prepared to be short of staff; good CISOs use cyber trustees.
- Educate the management and employees about threats; for a business to be resilient, everyone needs to be engaged in the journey.
- Perseverance and determination are needed for cyber defenders to succeed.

How does this advice relate to cyber emergencies and incident response? We often miss important trends, lessons learned (with many more coming in the next chapter), and insights that connect the dots when we are too close to a given situation.

Even after your organization and cybersecurity team have gone back over incidents and completed a "hot wash" where you reviewed the good, the bad, and the ugly, it can still be helpful for the leaders to compare notes with a trusted mentor who will offer new perspectives, connections, and improvements to your playbooks and response plans and strategy.

CHAPTER **11**

Turning Cyber Incident Lemons into Organizational Lemonade

Never let a good crisis go to waste.

–Winston Churchill

The BBC headline told a grim story: "Cyber-Attack on Irish Health Service 'Catastrophic.'"[1] The article began: "Health Service Executive (HSE) chief executive Paul Reid criticized the ransomware attack as a 'callous act' and an attack on health workers.

"The number of appointments in some areas of the system has dropped by 80%.

"Health workers are attempting to continue with paper records while work continues to recover IT systems. . . .

"However he said work to undo the damage will continue into the coming weeks. . . ."

Although the Conti ransomware group asked for $20 million to restore service, they suddenly handed over the decryption software tool for free, just under a week after the incident started.

"On its darknet website, the Conti ransomware group told the Health Service Executive (HSE), which runs Ireland's healthcare system, that 'we are providing the decryption tool for your network for

169

free. But you should understand that we will sell or publish a lot of private data if you will not connect us and try to resolve the situation.'"[2]

During that same week in May 2021, other hospitals in New Zealand and San Diego, California, were hit with ransomware, and we learned of attacks on education systems, local governments, and more. But even in the midst of an unrelenting surge in global ransomware cyberattacks, *Politico*'s Weekly Cybersecurity Newsletter closed with a message of optimism: "Not all hope is lost: There's plenty organizations can implement quickly to protect themselves from ransomware, such as regularly backing up data, using air gapped machines and creating offline, password-protected backup copies of information."[3]

ARE WE LEARNING FROM THESE TRUE STORIES?

Skeptics will no doubt say that these global organizations knew plenty of cyber best practices before these cyberattacks. So why do these increasingly scary cyber emergency stories proliferate? How can we take these substantial extortion and other technology security incident examples (call them lemons) and find some organizational good out of them (call that lemonade)?

What factors contribute to inadequate security protections, process failures, and worse? How can we get more clarity around implementing risk-reducing solutions – even after comprehensive risk assessments point to the areas that need attention?

Most organizations have (at least some) cyber best practices, international security standard practices, cyber framework guidelines, enterprise plans, award-winning solutions, and more. Even if you don't possess these solution checklists, it's not very hard to find them.

But why are these practices not followed? What inhibits ongoing success, security culture change, or whatever it takes to stop the data breaches, disarm ransomware, react faster to incidents, and implant professional incident response plans?[4]

The answers vary depending upon who you listen to, but the following are a few perspectives:

- The *MIT Sloan Management Review* describes unrealistic management expectations, disagreements over what actually is a best practice, and hidden long-term costs as three of the reasons that best practices often fail to be implemented or last.[5] The author concludes that implementing more reasonable standard practices often makes sense.

- The *Harvard Business Review* says that best practices don't translate across different cultures.[6] So a best practice in the United States may not succeed in India or China. This creates imbalances with global organizations.

- IBM's *Security Intelligence* website discusses several hurdles as to why companies have not implemented basic best practices. One is that companies choose expediency over security, and the author points out that those who do are more than twice as likely to suffer a data breach. The perspectives point to Verizon's Security Index findings. "Only 1 in 7 companies has taken all four basic security precautions outlined in the Verizon report — changing default passwords, encrypting data transmitted over public networks, restricting access on a need-to-know basis and regularly testing security systems – and only 14 percent of respondents rated their current degree of protection as 'very effective.' Additionally, more than half (51 percent) of the 600 companies Verizon surveyed said they lack a public Wi-Fi policy. . . ."[7]

- *CIO Magazine* offers 10 common excuses that people give, as well as five solutions.[8] All hit home, and offer perhaps the most compelling explanations as to why so many vulnerabilities are not patched and holes in cybersecurity defenses are not addressed in ongoing ways.

More details are provided on each item in the article, but the following two charts outline the excuses and helpful actions, along with our tips.

10 Excuses Why Best Practices Are Not Implemented	Fact-Finding (FF) Questions	Tips to Help
We did not have the time.	*Where are we spending the bulk of our time? Are we allocating our time proportionately according to the criticality levels of risks?*	Project management team needed.
We could not afford it.	*Are there other areas we are spending our budget on that can be reallocated? How does our budget align with the company's strategy and business risk?*	Budget and resources must be prioritized.
Our company is different.	*How have we educated our stakeholders to raise their level of awareness? Have we looked for security advocates and champions within the different divisions to assist in influencing laterally and upward?*	So is every company. Culture and leadership are required.
The vendor told us it was not necessary.	*How are we cross-checking what our third parties are telling us? Are we responsible for our customer's data and trust at the end of the day, or do we hold them entirely responsible?*	Ask: Who, what, when, where, how?

10 Excuses Why Best Practices Are Not Implemented	Fact-Finding (FF) Questions	Tips to Help
We didn't trust our system vendor.	*How do we scale the business in the future with growing partners and vendors if we don't have a system of keeping track of how our critical data is being shared? How are we assessing the maturity of our vendors' security posture?*	Excellence in contract management and ideally a framework to assess criticality of risks across the different vendor partnerships are needed.
We didn't understand why it was necessary.	*What is the current security awareness culture like among the leadership team and the different divisions?*	Team education is an ongoing must-have.
It was too hard.	*Have you tried getting allies so that it is not just you fighting an organizational battle? Are there other battles that might result in better outcomes? What are some other smaller initial commitments you can focus on securing from your stakeholders first, and then working your way on getting more buy-in from there?*	Time and resources + priority and follow-through required.

(Continued)

(Continued)

10 Excuses Why Best Practices Are Not Implemented	Fact-Finding (FF) Questions	Tips to Help
We tried this before and it didn't work.	*What was the environment like before when it didn't work? What were the reasons it failed? How can change be made and executed differently this time? Have you looked at the mechanics of influence?*	The right time, place, product, team, and culture are needed for success – it may be best to try again.
We were afraid of what we might discover.	*Are you comfortable with not knowing what the malicious attackers out there know about your company? How are you managing your risks if you do not know what needs to be managed?*	Ongoing risk assessments are a must. Cyber risks do not just stop at us; we have to think about our customers too.
We thought we had a better way.	*Have you consulted the right opinions before coming to a decision? If an incident should happen and the company comes under scrutiny, is there documented evidence that due diligence has been done?*	Choose strategy wisely – with backup data.

Solutions

5 Things to Do About "Best Practice Apathy"	Tips to Help	Food for Thought
Make failure real	Exercises are a must – practice, practice, practice.	*What is your mindset, and what is leadership's view on cyber failures? Who is accountable? How can you build a culture and work environment that does not finger-point or blame, but encourages transparency in sharing lessons learned and mistakes owned?*
Failure Mode Effects Analysis (FMEA)	Create a structured process.	*Do you know what your industry peers are using? How does your process benchmark against theirs?*
Early identification of business operational continuity measures	Regular reports on readiness to management.	*What has been the impact on other organizations who do not have a BCP? How does your BCP compare in your industry sector? What are the different lessons learned each time it is being run?*
Methodology change control	What is the process? Refine, improve, and test.	*How often have you reviewed your process? Are there ways of doing this more effectively?*

(Continued)

(Continued)

5 Things to Do About "Best Practice Apathy"	Tips to Help	Food for Thought
Get a second opinion	Constantly be looking to improve. Third-party experts can provide a fresh look.	*We are stronger together. How can you play on your strengths while leveraging the community or collaborating with existing or new partnerships to complement and strengthen your business case?*

A few additional thoughts on the "make failure real" suggestion in the chart. Many CISOs say that they would love a leadership job right *after* a major data breach or headline-grabbing security incident strikes an organization.

Why? Because the last security leader got the boot, and you can come in with a new sense of urgency, additional resources (often more people and dollars), and very low overall career risk, because everyone knows the data breach just happened and it was not the new CISO's fault.

The challenge becomes how to get that sense of urgency before a major, expensive data breach or emergency cyber incident that is known.

One answer is to ensure that current (lower level, nonemergency) cyber incidents and vulnerabilities are being communicated to senior management in repeatable ways. Stories of supply chain and competitor data breaches are often effective at grabbing the attention of top decision makers.

While all of these lists offer pragmatic, common-sense reasons that change does not occur or last in public and private sector companies, there is another reason near the top of the list: the belief that "it won't happen to us."

While this may seem very conceited, shortsighted, or even incredible to some, overconfidence is commonplace. See Chapter 10 for more on this leadership blind spot.

Finally, should organizations worry if they are using the wrong list of best practices? Some have argued that global data breaches are occurring at unprecedented levels because we are doing the wrong things.

One author even states: "The hacking at Colonial Pipeline is the latest in a series of breaches that have impacted a long-and-growing list of other businesses – all ambushed by some individual or group that managed to hack through cyber security 'industry best practices . . .'"[9]

The trouble is that in most cases, and with the Colonial Pipeline breach in particular, best practices were not being followed in all areas, based on public reports of system vulnerabilities.[10]

The main point is that you should choose a well-documented, reputable set of standards and cyber best practices to follow and do so with rigor. (The NIST Cyber Framework is one example.)

While it is certainly worthwhile and important to try to adopt an excellent framework that consistently addresses the appropriate people, processes, and technology, including cyber controls, tools, protections, and staffing to secure your organization's critical data assets, data breaches generally occur via a weak link where best-practice lists were not followed consistently.

CALLS FOR MORE RESILIENCE AND DOING MUCH BETTER

The U.S. RSA Conference has been the largest annual cybersecurity conference in the world for many years. In 2021, due to the COVID-19 pandemic, the conference was a virtual-only event, and several presentations provided short testimonials on resilience in cybersecurity. These brief, passionate testimonials, which are available for free on YouTube,[11] offer a glimpse of many lessons learned during a time of immense change and online uncertainty.

Chloé Messdaghi, cofounder of WoSEC and Hacking is NOT a crime, and founder of WeAreHackerz, reflected on the importance of being present and engaged in the moment, and not just focusing on planning for projects and events one, two, or three years out.[12] She exclaimed, "The pandemic put everything on hold, which made me realize and recognize that there will be times when you do not have control of your own life."

That same sentiment applies to cyber emergency incident responses for everyone involved as responders to emergency situations. There is a need to block out all other distractions, plans, and projects that were thought to be important before the incident, and focus on the actions required at that moment in incident response. There is a need to adapt to new circumstances and work together in newly formed teams to accomplish a very specific mission.

Another vital perspective on the "urgency of the moment and the need for us to renew our commitment to partnership" came from Anne Neuberger, Deputy National Security Advisor for Cyber and Emerging Technology in the Biden Administration. She spoke about not only the national security perspectives regarding cybersecurity, but an economic security imperative as well.[13]

Neuberger cited several lessons from the SolarWinds incident:

1. Adversaries will look for any opening to attack.
2. Partnerships are critical to the safety of our nation in cyberspace.
3. Governments need to urgently modernize cybersecurity defenses. To do this, we must shift our mindset from incident response to prevention by getting ahead of threats and facilitate early detection.

She elaborated on what it means to shift our mindset: "I've observed as a community, we've accepted that we'll move from one incident response to the next. And while we must acknowledge breaches will happen, and prepare for them, we simply cannot let 'waiting for the next shoe to drop' to be the status quo under which we operate. The national security implications of doing so are too grave."

She describes "three complementary and mutually reinforcing lines of effort":

1. Modernize cyber defenses.
2. Return to a more active role on cyber internationally.
3. Ensure America's better posture to compete.

In the area of protecting critical infrastructure, Neuberger described new private sector efforts with the energy industry to install new technologies that provide timely visibility, detection, response, and blocking capabilities. These steps will "protect the technologies upon which our critical services depend."

MORE LESSONS LEARNED

After every headline-grabbing cyberattack, there are almost always lists of lessons learned and takeaways. Some thoughts are certainly better than others. Edward Segal, a crisis management expert and author of *Crisis Ahead: 101 Ways to Prepare for and Bounce Back from Disasters, Scandals, and Other Emergencies*, offered "7 Crisis Management Lessons From Colonial Pipeline's Response To Cyber Attack" in *Forbes*.[14]

These lessons include:

1. Tell people what happened.
2. Call in the experts.
3. Establish priorities.
4. Don't speculate.
5. Take control.
6. Send the right message.
7. Isolate the problem.

This practice of learning from major security incidents, including how your team responds, is not new. However, the lessons learned are (sadly) often forgotten.

After the huge data breach at SolarWinds, the World Economic Forum published four ways that global governments and businesses can work together to be more effective in cybersecurity defenses.[15] Those items included:

1. Share threat intelligence.
2. Align cyber education with market needs.
3. Sharpen incident-response capabilities.
4. Build security by design.

For item 3, they recommend:

"Even the best cyber defense is likely to be cracked. That's why effective organizations have well-rehearsed plans in place to deal with attackers.

"Several nations provide forums where government and business collaborate in response to cyberattacks. In the United States, CISA's National Cyber Incident Response Plan defines cyber defense as a 'shared responsibility' of individuals, the private sector, and government; spells out the roles government departments will play in responding to attacks; and commits federal officials to safeguarding the privacy and intellectual property of companies.[16] The UK's National Cyber Security Centre, an arm of the GCHQ intelligence agency,[17] coordinates similar responses and sets out which private sector cyber specialists it will collaborate with. . . ."

In a 2013 example, ISSA presented a seminar entitled "Life's A Breach Report: Making Lemonade Out of Lemons."[18] Pete Lindstrom, who was the Principal at Spire Security at that time, offered five questions to ask yourself after a breach, along with actions to help. It is still relevant in the 2020s and beyond.

Question	Action
1. How much did you lose?	Calculate (or at least estimate) losses.
2. What was the source of the attack?	Identify/monitor your attack vectors.
3. Was your response efficient/effective?	Assess security spending.
4. Were you negligent or "unlucky"?	Measure/assess risk levels.
5. Where and when will the next attack take place?	Use metrics to support risk management.

BACK TO THE BEGINNING: A CIRCULAR APPROACH TO INCIDENT RESPONSE DURING CYBER EMERGENCIES

The NIST Cybersecurity Framework (CSF) is designed to reduce risk by improving the management of cybersecurity risk. The CSF offers a diagram that articulates the five functions: identify, protect, detect, respond, and recover (see Figure 11.1).

Furthermore, under the fifth area of recovery, NIST describes the need to make improvements to processes, procedures, and technologies.[19]

Which brings us full circle to preparing for the next incident based on the lessons learned from past incidents and exercises. There are several formal methodologies for capturing these lessons to make "lemonade out of lemons," and one of those is a "hot wash" procedure, as described in the Cyberstorm examples earlier.

NIST 800-84 is the "Guide to Test, Training, and Exercise Programs for IT Plans and Capabilities." Pages 5–6 include this important point:

During the evaluation phase, the exercise director relies on the design team or other specified staff to develop the after action report that documents findings and recommendations from the

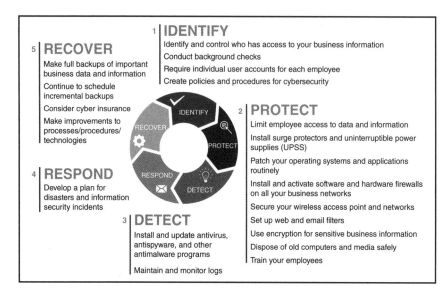

FIGURE 11.1
Source: NIST, https://www.nist.gov/sites/default/files/styles/960_x_960_limit/public/images/2018/05/01/cybersecurity-flyer-graphic.png?itok=yjdnk5Re.

functional exercise. Exercise notes, forms, and other material created during the course of exercise play and during the hotwash are the basis of the after action report. The introduction to the after action report should document background information about the exercise such as the scope, objectives, and scenario. The after action report should also document observations made by the exercise staff and participants during the exercise and recommendations for enhancing the IT plan that was exercised. The after action report should also include a list of exercise participants and may provide information from any participant surveys that were distributed during the hotwash to solicit feedback.

Following the development of the after action report, the plan coordinator might assign action items to select personnel in an effort to update the IT plan being exercised. The plan coordinator should then update the plan, if appropriate, by implementing recommendations made in the after action report. It may also be necessary to brief certain managers on the results of the exercise, update other security-related documents, and perform other actions based on the exercise. . . .[20]

Following is one simple example from a hospital's cyber incident.

A HELPFUL HOSPITAL EXAMPLE

In October 2020 a small, rural hospital in Michigan's Upper Peninsula was the victim of a ransomware attack. On a Saturday afternoon, when the chief compliance and risk officer received a voicemail indicating that systems were down, she assumed that the cause was a routine hardware or software failure that would soon be rectified. It wasn't until the second phone call that she learned that a ransom note had been discovered.

The attack against this small rural hospital disrupted systems and communications for weeks and made it difficult to treat patients and perform routine hospital functions. IT systems were down, so patient care reverted to paper; simple functions like getting insurance authorizations reverted to phone calls; and for the first time ever, the hospital had staff physically driving to pick up patient medical records from other providers. The event put a strain on the health system and the communities it serves.

MAKING LEMONADE

Fortunately, the attack and its effects were an opportunity in disguise. The attack rallied support and reiterated the criticality of information security and IT. Despite the stress on the organization, they were responsive to the attack and eager to improve their security posture.

They hired Doug Copley, the former CISO from Beaumont Hospital in Michigan, to run their security program. Doug's enterprise experience, industry connections, and focus on helping smaller organizations with cyber preparedness fit well with this small rural healthcare entity's ideal.

Taking input from the forensics investigators and taking advice from the Michigan Cyber Command Center and the FBI, at the time of Doug's entrance to the organization, activities were already underway to enhance firewall protections, endpoint detection and response, and security monitoring. Despite all the security controls in place, Doug wanted a better way to tie all the controls together. Over the next several months, he focused on adopting industry frameworks and putting a comprehensive security roadmap in place. Within months the hospital security team had instituted the NIST 800-53 and NIST CSF frameworks, worked through a new security risk assessment, and laid out a roadmap to mature the information security functions. The attack was disruptive and stressful, but it was important to harness the heightened focus from leadership to drive advancement into the information security program.

FIVE LESSONS FROM THE HOSPITAL ATTACK

Doug shared several lessons learned as a result of this attack.

1. Advanced antimalware is a necessity. With the continual advancement in cyberattack methods, it is critically important to have strong detection and response capabilities on every device possible.
2. Leverage machine learning in security monitoring. The volume of events to monitor can be staggering, and machines can monitor events much more quickly than humans. Leverage automated monitoring so anomalies can be identified and escalated faster.
3. System dependencies sometimes lie *outside* your organization. It's important that your Business Impact Assessment (BIA) clearly

articulate *all* dependencies, even with third parties. When security incidents cause you to sever communications with third parties, it will take time and energy to convince them to re-enable communications.

4. Continuity and recovery plans must be accessible. Maintain copies in paper format or on secure cloud platforms that can be accessed when company systems are down.

5. Practice, practice, practice. Although they may not prepare you 100% for attacks, running periodic exercises to educate team members on proper incident protocols can help ensure that people follow procedures in times of crisis.

FIVE LESSONS FROM DIVERSE INFORMATION SHARING AND ANALYSIS CENTERS (ISACs)

Carlos P. Kizzee has worked in a variety of senior leadership capacities, including director and executive VP roles with several ISACS and senior roles within the U.S. Department of Homeland Security (DHS). Carlos's observations of many organizations responding to cyber incidents have provided some key differentiators between those who do well and those who do not.

"The first differentiator is the organization's commitment to peer engagement and collaboration. I am not just talking about information sharing here, I'm talking about meaningful peer interaction. Organizations who are in the habit of active and proactive peer engagement have a means to detect earlier, to be aware of, and to embrace the most relevant security controls and best practices. This helps them to enhance detection and prevention efforts and to shorten the time to mitigation. These organizations evidence the commitment to learn from and with their peers *before* there is a problem, and to leverage security collaboration to give them an edge.

"The next differentiator is the organization's ability to prioritize risk management efforts. No enterprise can eliminate all risk. Resources are limited, and the identification of new and emerging threats and vulnerabilities is continuous. Organizations who have internal mechanisms and capabilities that focus security activities to what matters most to their enterprise evidence best practices in prioritizing threat detection and vulnerability management activities against relevant risks and key organizational concerns. This places them ahead of their peers.

"A third standout is the organization's dedication to cybersecurity fundamentals. Every security vendor will confirm that their latest shiny ball capability is all that is needed to meet the next great security concern. It is wise to keep an eye on emerging capabilities and evaluate what works, but it is essential to keep the team focused on enhancing their efforts in the fundamentals. Patching, tuning and implementation of tools for highest efficacy, and maintaining and enhancing key analyst and operational tradecraft should be a priority. Organizations must be dedicated to not being distracted by every new, latest thing to the detriment of their focus on the fundamentals.

"Fourth among the key differentiators of quality organizations is the commitment to meaningful security. Organizations should not be satisfied with the 'security kabuki' of looking secure or achieving milestones in security effort while hiding actual risks and key controls behind masks and layers of greasepaint. Organizations need to focus on applying controls in depth that are essential to their security, and to promoting an alert and security-aware workforce that is mature and sincere in key habits of cyber hygiene that are informed by the threats of aggressive and highly motivated threat actors, and by the priorities of their organization and its overall mission.

"Fifth and final among differentiators is an organization's commitment to its people. Leaders who invest in their people's training, their quality of life, and who remember that they compete with their employee's next, best green grass employment opportunity will care for their people so that their security workforce can stay sharp, focused, and motivated to their critical tasks."

BRINGING IT ALL TOGETHER

Throughout the chapters, we have explored and peeled off the layers of different approaches taken by industry experts in preparing and managing crises.

Cyberattacks will only continue, with cybercrime presently being forecasted as a $6 trillion industry,[21] and $10.5 trillion by 2025.[22] Put into context, the drug trade is less than a $1 trillion business, although drug dealers are now resorting to cybercrime as detection is low and returns are high. And IoT is a rapidly growing industry, with 75 billion IoT devices connected to the virtual environment.[23] This only serves to present more threats, opportunities, and vulnerabilities for people.

Historically, communities have had the perspective that as long as virtual crimes are out of sight, the threat is out of mind. Unfortunately, COVID-19 has revealed more recent real-world impact, as seen with the attempted manipulation of pandemic information, vaccines, and even elections.

As we see global problems start to emerge relating to access to water, food and vaccines, and so on, people will turn to alternative methods to survive. Throughout the book, we have seen the many devastating consequences of cyber crime being turned into a paid-for-service activity, including the economizing of people's suffering, as in the case of the cyber incident at the hospital.

In a Mega C-Suite Stories podcast with Doug Witschi, assistant director of Interpol's Cybercrime Threat Response, he shared his view that cyber crime presents a global threat to the global industry, and a global problem needs a global solution.[24]

"We have over 200 countries globally that set their own laws, set their own policies, and resource the government capabilities that provide a government response to some of the threats that we're seeing around cybercrime. Each country has their own thoughts and ideas about what's right and what's wrong, based on a range of different mechanisms and issues.

"I think the challenge for a global crime type such as this is the lack of consistency. And that lack of consistency also inadvertently provides protections for organized criminals. You'll have countries that are strong in certain elements in relation to cyber crime, and the neighboring country won't have any laws whatsoever. What's to stop a person from actually stepping across a border and being 'provided' an element of protection or untouchability and continuing to exploit the same criminal activities on victims on the other side of the world?

"We've had a case where we had a target that we identified; we got in touch with one of the primary countries that was a victim of that target. And now we're reluctant to bring them back into that jurisdiction for prosecution, because the chance of them getting any jail time for their crimes was next to zero."

Witschi draws the opposite comparison with the country that they've identified this target in, where it was most likely that they would get mandatory jail time for the crimes that they committed. He brought to light the irony that in one country, a theft of tens or hundreds of thousands of dollars is considered a criminal offense, while another country may not impose any penalty at all.

Global crime ignores boundaries. Laws are complex, and it can take years before someone is prosecuted. Geopolitics also play a big part in how Interpol treads carefully in addressing threats. We need to be more agile in threat response and in prosecution.

Witschi believes that over time, these gaps will start to minimize and be mitigated, also in relation to powers and authorities that various governments provide to have law enforcement respond, prosecute, or impose penalties for those activities.

THE ECOSYSTEM VIEW

To fight cybercrime at a global scale, countries need to partner with other countries. Partnering is more than just partnering with the law enforcement; alliances need to be formed with the banks, cybersecurity firms, supply chains, transport, oil, and gas across diverse sectors.

Witschi explained, "The challenge for us as part of an international community, in the virtual environment, is that a cyberattack on one is a cyberattack on all. For us as a global ecosystem, we need to actually start to come together and work a lot more diligently and collaboratively. Yes, politics plays a part in some of the discussions that we have across geopolitical environments. But at the end of the day, we're chasing criminals. We're chasing people that try to exploit other people and take advantage of other people."

LEADING BY EXAMPLE

The greatest challenge in collaborating with law enforcement is the issue of trust. The truth is that people simply do not like to report cyber crime.

In the event of a data breach, they are worried about their risk to their bottom line. It is never ideal to pay a ransom, which ultimately rewards criminals for their activities and behaviors. However, the truth is that when business livelihoods, the livelihoods of the people who work within the organization, are at stake, it presents interesting challenges and issues for the organization to take certain actions. Should they choose to pay a ransom, then it's less likely that they're going to report the incident. Also, they're probably not agreeable to sharing that information more broadly, which feeds back into the cycle and extrapolates underreporting.

In just a span of a few weeks as we finished writing this book, we have seen many ransomware attacks on big corporations that have grabbed national and international headlines. From the suffering going on in Ireland's health service to the gas pipelines in the United States and JBS meat services in the United States and Australia, it hits home for Witschi. He explained that targeting these threats and trying to get a response around them is a real issue of actively engaging with nations. "Sometimes, we can't get the priority because they haven't got an identified number of threats, risks, or issues that they've identified within this jurisdiction. And one of those is the reporting element."

A case in point: Through one of their private–public partnerships, Interpol identified thousands of victims in a country facing a ransomware attack. "When we advised that country that they had an issue with that ransomware strain, they told us that they only had two reports. They were surprised when we provided them with a list of more than 11,000 victims. They then acknowledged that they had an issue and it became a priority for them to respond to that." As the victims were not reporting, naturally this hadn't been prioritized by law enforcements.

At a dinner Witschi attended in Singapore, a guest revealed that her company had been attacked by ransomware. He got the name of the company, went back to the office to make some inquiries, and identified the ransomware. Apparently, the attack had started 10 days earlier. Interpol reached out to the country where the company was headquartered and offered their assistance because they had a decrypter for that specific ransomware. The problem was solved in a matter of minutes, as opposed to a delay of many weeks.

Problems and issues need to be shared so that they can be remediated properly. "Dare to share" was the catchphrase the team came up with for sharing intelligence and identifying information that may help in preventing, disrupting, or apprehending the targets behind these threats.

Additionally, when a company is able to talk through their threats publicly, this bolsters confidence within the industry for others to likewise share the threats they have faced as well.

This is an issue that won't be solved overnight; however, if the community plays their part in plugging the gaps, and nations look beyond the geopolitical affairs focusing on solely global crimes, cooperation across the different countries could achieve more effective outcomes.

Interpol is one example of an organization that has a cyber threat response capability and is progressing in making a difference for their current 194 member countries. With strong private–public partnerships across the globe, they have been able to provide immediate responses to ransomware attacks on telcos to financial crimes and even to the hospitals providing Covid support.

With more versatility in being able to shop for services from one country that another might not have, they have also brought in public partners for member countries that do not have a CERT, which aids in getting them up to speed.

Witschi explained, "We're all in this together, and we need to work out mechanisms to be able to expediently disrupt threats as they emerge to protect all our industry partners from these types of attacks. But we also need to look at how we can actually disrupt the threat actors, whether it's through the infrastructure they use, obviously, their livelihood, and the financial guys, they generally extrapolate out of these types of criminal activity. I think that's ultimately where we need to be. I think the challenge for a global community with a global crime type is we need to radically change how we may do this. What we need to do is try to get some sort of global consistency in relation to these standards."

We also need to continually think about improving the framework for global collaboration so that we can better protect our communities. Even from a law enforcement perspective, how do we act quickly in an international environment with domestic enforcement services? We need to influence people to think differently. The more our industry shares data with our community, CERTs, law enforcement, and Interpol, the more our ecosystem will level up and accelerate its progress in addressing cybercrime more effectively.

Despite geopolitical issues, collaboration remains a powerful key and solution to face any Cyber Mayday incidents in the future, head-on, with boldness, and because we are stronger together.

Free Cyber Incident Resources

Time is the scarcest resource and unless it is managed nothing else can be managed.

—Peter Drucker

CYBER INCIDENT RESPONSE PLANNING AND PLANS

Australia NSW Cyber Security Incident Emergency Management Sub Plan: https://www.emergency.nsw.gov.au/Documents/plans/sub-plans/cyber-security-incident-sub-plan.pdf

Crest Security Incident Response Guide – Version 1: https://www.crest-approved.org/wp-content/uploads/2014/11/CSIR-Procurement-Guide.pdf

Cynet Incident Response Plan Templates and Guide: https://www.cynet.com/incident-response/incident-response-plan-template/

GOsafeonline in Singapore incident response checklist: https://www.csa.gov.sg/gosafeonline/resources/incident-response-checklist?s=09

The National Cyber Incident Response Plan (NCIRP): https://us-cert.cisa.gov/ncirp

NIST Special Publication 800-61, revision 2, Computer Security Incident Handling Guide: https://nvlpubs.nist.gov/nistpubs/SpecialPublications/NIST.SP.800-61r2.pdf

STANDARDS, FRAMEWORKS, AND POLICIES

Australia's equivalent of FedRAMP – IRAP Security Framework: https://www.cyber.gov.au/acsc/view-all-content/programs/irap

Australian Government Information Security Manual (ISM): https://www.cyber.gov.au/acsc/view-all-content/ism

Australian Government Protective Security Policy Framework (PSPF): https://www.protectivesecurity.gov.au/

Comparison guide between NIST and SANS incident response processes: https://cybersecurity.att.com/blogs/security-essentials/incident-response-steps-comparison-guide

Cyber Operational Resilience Intelligence-led Exercises (CORIE) for Financial Institutions including Financial Market Infrastructure in Australia: https://www.cfr.gov.au/publications/policy-statements-and-other-reports/2020/corie-pilot-program-guideline/pdf/corie-framework-guideline.pdf

Diagram with five core functions of the NIST Cybersecurity Framework: https://www.nist.gov/cyberframework/online-learning/five-functions

The Health Insurance Portability and Accountability Act of 1996 (HIPAA): https://www.hhs.gov/hipaa/for-professionals/security/laws-regulations/index.html

HITRUST CSF (offers a way to comply with standards such as ISO/IEC 27000-series and HIPAA): https://hitrustalliance.net/

ISO/IEC 27001:2013: https://www.iso.org/standard/54534.html

Mitigation Strategies from Australian Cyber Security Centre – Australian Signals Directorate (ASD) Essential Eight: https://www.cyber.gov.au/acsc/view-all-content/essential-eight

MITRE ATT&CK® Mitigation: https://attack.mitre.org/mitigations/enterprise/ and https://attack.mitre.org/mitigations/mobile/

NIST Cybersecurity Framework: https://www.nist.gov/cyberframework/online-learning/history-and-creation-framework and https://www.nist.gov/cyberframework

Other Relevant NIST documents (https://csrc.nist.gov/publications/sp):

Guide for Developing the Risk Management Framework to Federal Information Systems: A Security Life Cycle Approach [NIST SP 800-37, Revision 1]

Guide to Integrating Forensic Techniques into Incident Response [NIST SP 800-86, Revision 2]

Guide to Malware Incident Prevention and Handling [NIST SP 800-83]

Guide to Test, Training, and Exercise Programs for IT Plans and Capabilities [NIST SP 800-84]

Information Security Continuous Monitoring for Federal Information Systems and Organizations [NIST SP 800-137]

Risk Management Guide for Information Technology Systems [NIST SP 800-30, Revision 1]

OWASP Top 10 Standard Awareness for Web Application Security Risks: https://owasp.org/www-project-top-ten/

Secure Cloud federal government – FedRAMP: https://www.fedramp.gov/

Secure Cloud state and local governments – StateRAMP: https://stateramp.org

SOC 2 Trust Services Criteria: https://www.aicpa.org/interestareas/frc/assuranceadvisoryservices/aicpasoc2report.html

Ten Steps to Cybersecurity (UK National Cyber Security Centre, GCHQ): https://www.ncsc.gov.uk/collection/10-steps

UK HMG Security Policy Framework: https://www.history.org.uk/files/download/7311/1294317994/SecurityPolicyFramework.pdf

UK National Cyber Security Centre (NCSC) Cyber Assessment Framework (CAF) guidance: https://www.ncsc.gov.uk/collection/caf

US-CERT Resources: https://us-cert.cisa.gov/resources/

EXERCISE TEMPLATES

Center for Internet Security's six free tabletop exercises: https://www.cisecurity.org/white-papers/six-tabletop-exercises-prepare-cybersecurity-team/

CISA Exercise support website: https://www.cisa.gov/national-cyber-exercise-and-planning-program

Cyber Storm 2020: https://www.cisa.gov/cyber-storm-2020

NIST Guide to Test, Training, and Exercise Programs for IT Plans and Capabilities [NIST SP 800-84]: https://nvlpubs.nist.gov/nistpubs/Legacy/SP/nistspecialpublication800-84.pdf

CYBER STRATEGY DOCUMENTS

Australia New South Wales Cyber Security Strategy: https://www.digital.nsw.gov.au/transformation/cyber-security/cyber-security-strategy

Cyber Security Policy, Mandatory Requirements: https://www.digital.nsw.gov.au/policy/cyber-security-policy/mandatory-requirements

CISA Cyber Incident Data and Analysis Working Group white papers: https://www.cisa.gov/publication/cyber-incident-data-and-analysis-working-group-white-papers

CISA Publications Library on Cybersecurity: https://www.cisa.gov/publications-library/Cybersecurity

Michigan Cyber Civilian Corps: https://www.michigan.gov/som/0,4669,7-192-78403_78404_78419---,00.html

Michigan Cyber Disruption Response Plan: https://www.michigan.gov/documents/cybersecurity/120815_Michigan_Cyber_Disruption_Response_Plan_Online_VersionA_507848_7.pdf

Michigan Cyber Initiative (2015): https://www.michigan.gov/documents/cybersecurity/Mich_Cyber_Initiative_11.13_2PM_web_474127_7.pdf

The National Association of State Chief Information Officers (NASCIO) Cyber Disruption Response Planning Guide: https://www.nascio.org/resource-center/resources/cyber-disruption-response-planning-guide/

National Governors Association (NGA) Issue Brief on State Cyber Disruption Response Plans: https://www.nga.org/wp-content/uploads/2019/04/IssueBrief_MG.pdf

Ransomware Task Force Plans: https://securityandtechnology.org/ransomwaretaskforce/report/

Singapore CSA Cyber Security Strategy: https://www.csa.gov.sg/news/publications/singapore-cybersecurity-strategy

INCIDENT RESPONSE PLAYBOOKS

American Public Power Association Cyber Incident Response Playbook: https://www.publicpower.org/system/files/documents/Public-Power-Cyber-Incident-Response-Playbook.pdf

Cyber Exercise Playbook, November 2014: https://www.mitre.org/sites/default/files/publications/pr_14-3929-cyber-exercise-playbook.pdf

"Cybersecurity Checklist to Protect Your Online Business: A Priority for MSMEs in Their Post-COVID Digital Transformation": https://www.entrepreneur.com/article/372206

Incident Response Playbook Designer: https://www.incidentresponse.com/playbooks/

Instructions on Incident Notification and Reporting to Monetary Authority of Singapore (MAS), including Incident Responding Template: https://www.mas.gov.sg/regulation/forms-and-templates/instructions-on-incident-notification-and-reporting-to-mas

"Microsoft Releases Free Online 'Playbooks' to Help Businesses Defend against Cyber-attacks": https://portswigger.net/daily-swig/microsoft-releases-online-playbooks-to-help-businesses-defend-against-cyber-attacks

CERT RESOURCES

Asia Pacific CERT: https://www.apcert.org/

Australia ACSC Alerts for Individuals & Families, Small & Medium Businesses, Large Organisations & Infrastructure, and Government: https://www.cyber.gov.au/acsc/view-all-content/alerts

UK CERT: http://www.ukcert.org.uk/

US CERT: https://us-cert.cisa.gov/resources

Assessments: Cyber Resilience Review (CRR): https://us-cert.cisa.gov/resources/assessments

Cybersecurity Framework: https://us-cert.cisa.gov/resources/cybersecurity-framework

Industrial Control Systems (Alerts, Advisories, Reports): https://us-cert.cisa.gov/ics

Related Resources (including security organizations, vulnerability information, tools techniques, research and guidelines, education, Information Sharing & Analysis Centers (ISACs), and more: https://us-cert.cisa.gov/related-resources

Resources for Academia: https://us-cert.cisa.gov/resources/academia

Resources for Business: https://us-cert.cisa.gov/resources/business

Resources for Federal Government: https://us-cert.cisa.gov/resources/federal

Resources for Small and Midsize Businesses (SMB): https://us-cert.cisa.gov/resources/smb

Resources for State, Local, Tribal, and Territorial (SLTT) Governments: https://us-cert.cisa.gov/resources/sltt

CYBER INSURANCE GUIDANCE

CISA, "Cybersecurity Insurance": https://www.cisa.gov/cyber-security-insurance

"Demystifying Cyber Insurance Coverage," Deloitte University Press: https://www2.deloitte.com/content/dam/Deloitte/nl/Documents/financial-services/deloitte-nl-fsi-demystifying-cyber-insurance-coverage-report.pdf

NGA, "States Confront the Cyber Challenge: Cyber Liability Insurance for States": https://www.nga.org/wp-content/uploads/2019/09/Cybersecurity-Insurance-Two-Pager-Final.pdf

LESSONS LEARNED DOCUMENTS

FEMA, Lessons Learned on Information Sharing Covering the Michigan Cyber Disruption Response Strategy: https://cip.gmu.edu/wp-content/uploads/2015/11/nps73-090514-05.pdf

ICT SCRM Task Force: Lessons Learned During the COVID-19 Pandemic Report: https://www.cisa.gov/publication/ict-supply-chain-lessons-learned-covid-19

"Innovate For Cyber Resilience: Lessons from Leaders to Master Cybersecurity Execution," Accenture Security, 2020: https://www.accenture.com/_acnmedia/PDF-116/Accenture-Cybersecurity-Report-2020.pdf

TRAINING OPPORTUNITIES, INCLUDING CYBER RANGES

IBM Cyber Range: https://www.ibm.com/security/services/ managed-security-services/command-center-mobile

"Introducing the Michigan Cyber Range," *Government Technology*, November 12, 2012. https://www.govtech.com/blogs/ lohrmann-on-cybersecurity/introducing-the-michigan-cyber-111212.html

Merit description of Alphaville and Griffinville inside Michigan Cyber Range: https://www.merit.edu/security/training/alphaville/

Michigan Cyber Range: https://en.wikipedia.org/wiki/Michigan_ Cyber_Range and https://www.merit.edu/security/training/hubs/

Palo Alto Networks Cyber Range: https://www.paloaltonetworks. com/solutions/initiatives/cyberrange-overview

U.S. Cyber Range at Virginia Tech: https://www.uscyberrange.org/

Virginia Cyber Range: https://www.virginiacyberrange.org/

LAWS AND REPORTING ON DATA BREACHES AND PROTECTING DATA

Data Protection Trustmark (DPTM) enterprise-wide certification: https://www.imda.gov.sg/programme-listing/data-protection-trustmark-certification

The EU General Data Protection Regulation (GDPR): https:// gdpr.eu/

Personal Data Protection Act (PDPA) for Singapore: https:// www.pdpc.gov.sg/Overview-of-PDPA/The-Legislation/ Personal-Data-Protection-Act

State-specific data breach reporting laws as listed by the National Conference of State Legislatures:

Data Breach Reporting Laws in a map: https://www.itgovern-anceusa.com/data-breach-notification-laws

Montana: Reported Data Breach Incidents: https://dojmt.gov/consumer/databreach/

CRISIS COMMUNICATIONS

"Breaking Bad News with CONSOLE: Toward a Framework Integrating Medical Protocols with Crisis Communication," https://www.sciencedirect.com/science/article/pii/S0363811117303697

Crisis Ready Institute Issue Management Response Flowchart: https://crisisreadyinstitute.com/crisis-ready-resource-for-you-issue-management-response-flowchart/

"The Four Steps to Creating the Ultimate Crisis Comms Plan," Cision: https://www.cision.ca/content/dam/cision-ca/resources/white-papers/2020-Q1-Crisis-Comms-COVID-19-CA.pdf

"Reimagining Crisis Communications," Pinkston: https://pinkston.co/reimagining-crisis-communications

Acknowledgments

Dan Lohrmann: I would like to thank the amazing team that helped bring this book together, starting with the industry thought leaders who provided personal stories, lessons learned, and best practices to share, especially Bill Nash, Doug Copley, Deb Snyder, Earl Duby, Kevin Ford, Carlos Kizzee, Scott Larsen, Mark Stamford, Mike Davis, Nancy Rainosek, Mark Weatherford, and Renault Ross. Your insights and frontline experiences battling cyberattacks bring emergency cyber incidents to life for readers. You're the best, and I greatly appreciate your contributions to this book.

Special recognition is due to the great team at Wiley, starting with our editor, Julie Kerr, who greatly improved our manuscript. Thanks go out to Chloé Miller-Bess, Dawn Kilgore, Jeanenne Ray, Philo Antonie Mahendran, and Sally Baker, who made the book possible.

An extra-special thanks to my coauthor, Shamane Tan, who is passionate, faithful, kind, and has been a true joy to work with throughout this journey.

I would also like to thank my wife Priscilla and my family, who always encourage and support my writing. You light up my life.

Finally, I would like to thank God, who has granted me countless blessings, knowledge, and the unique opportunity to write this book with Shamane.

Shamane Tan: There are plenty of people who helped bring this book to fruition, and I am grateful to all of them. Thank you especially to this generation of leaders who took the time to share their stories and experiences with me as well as giving back to our community. Special thanks to Steve Katz, Gregory J. Touhill, King Lee, John Yates, Theo

Nassiokas, Yuval Illuz, Doug Witschi, Preston Miller, Ang Leong Boon, Shao Fei Huang, Venkatesh Subramaniam, Kevin Kok-Yew Tan, Todd Carroll, Doron Sivan, Michael Cracroft, and Melissa Agnes.

To our incredible industry leaders and readers who are passionately fighting against cyber crisis at the frontlines and striving to make the world around us a safer place, this is for you. I would also like to express my thanks to my wonderful Cyber Risk Meetup community and partners who have rallied behind, supported, and inspired me over the years. Chris Cubbage, Ian Yip, Daniel Barratt, Cindi Wirawan, Vivienne Mutembwa and Nokan Konan, you are but a few special friends who have been integral in my many milestones. I also cannot forget my Privasec | Sekuro team, especially Romain Rallu, Prashant Haldankar, and Karan Khosla – your heart for our industry and passion for security have taught me much.

A huge shout-out to my coauthor, Dan Lohrmann, for his passion, wisdom, and amazing energy. It is God-incidental that our paths crossed years ago when I was writing my first book. To our editor Julie Kerr, thank you for your most excellent help, and to the Wiley publishing team – Jeanenne Ray, Sally Baker, Dawn Kilgore, Philo Antonie Mahendran, and Chloé Miller-Bess – it has been an absolute pleasure working on this book together with this dream team.

Finally, I would like to thank my mum, dad, my two younger brothers, special loved ones, and dear friends, who have always cheered me on in any of my endeavors – my world is bright because you are in it. Above all, I am most grateful to God for His love and favor that I have experienced throughout this journey.

About the Authors

Daniel J. Lohrmann is an internationally recognized cybersecurity leader, technologist, keynote speaker, blogger, and author. Having started his career at the National Security Agency (NSA), Dan has also served global technology and security teams with Lockheed Martin (formerly Loral Aerospace), ManTech International, the state of Michigan, and Security Mentor, Inc. He has received numerous executive leadership awards, including *SC Magazine* CSO of the Year, *Governing* Public Official of the Year, *Computerworld* Premier 100 IT Leader, and *Cybersecurity Breakthrough* CISO of the Year.

Dan is the author of two books, *Virtual Integrity: Faithfully Navigating the Brave New Web* and *BYOD for You: The Guide to Bring Your Own Device to Work*, and has contributed to numerous others. He has been a keynote speaker at global security and technology conferences from South Africa to Dubai and Washington, D.C. to Moscow.

Dan serves on advisory boards for cybersecurity nonprofit organizations, university information assurance (IA) programs, and cyber startup companies. He holds a master's degree in computer science (CS) from Johns Hopkins University and a bachelor's degree in CS from Valparaiso University.

As one of the most established women in the fields of technology and cybersecurity, **Shamane Tan** is the chief growth officer at Privasec, leading the security outreach strategy with the C-Suite and executives.

Known for her passion in spearheading industry awareness initiatives, Shamane has been recognized by IFSEC as one of the global top 20 cybersecurity influencers. She is the author of *Cyber Risk Leaders: Global C-Suite Insights – Leadership & Influence in the Cyber Age.*

In 2021, Shamane was given the Top 30 Women in Security ASEAN Region award after being named one of the 40 under 40 Most Influential Asian-Australians in 2020; she also received the Highly Commended award by the Australian Women in Security Network as the One to Watch. She has been a judge for numerous ceremonies and was a global judge for the Las Vegas Cybersecurity Women of the Year Award. Shamane is a sought-after TEDx speaker, international keynoter, and podcaster. She is the founder of Cyber Risk Meetup, an international community and platform for cyber risk executives to exchange learnings. She holds a bachelor's degree (Hons) in computer engineering from Nanyang Technological University in Singapore.

Notes

INTRODUCTION

1. President Joe Biden speech, quoted in Maggie Miller, "Biden: US Taking 'Urgent' Steps to Improve Cybersecurity," *The Hill*, February 4, 2021, https://thehill.com/policy/cybersecurity/537436-biden-says-administration-launching-urgent-initiative-to-improve-nations.
2. "Jerome Powell: Full 2021 60 Minutes Interview Transcript," 60 Minutes, April 11, 2021, https://www.cbsnews.com/news/jerome-powell-full-2021-60-minutes-interview-transcript/.
3. "Prepared Statement of Kevin Mandia, CEO of FireEye, Inc. before the United States Senate Select Committee on Intelligence," February 23, 2021, https://www.intelligence.senate.gov/sites/default/files/documents/os-kmandia-022321.pdf.
4. "Testimony of Microsoft President Brad Smith before the United States Senate Select Committee on Intelligence," February 23, 2021, https://www.intelligence.senate.gov/sites/default/files/documents/os-bsmith-022321.pdf.
5. "Written Testimony of Sudhakar Ramakrishna, Chief Executive Office, SolarWinds Inc. before the United States Senate Select Committee on Intelligence," February 23, 2021, https://www.intelligence.senate.gov/sites/default/files/documents/os-sramakrishna-022321.pdf.
6. "Testimony of the Federal Chief Information Security Officer Christopher J. DeRusha, United States Senate Homeland Security and Governmental Affairs," March 18, 2021, https://www.hsgac.senate.gov/imo/media/doc/Testimony-DeRusha-2021-03-18.pdf.
7. Gloria Gonzalez, Ben Lefebvre, and Eric Geller, "'Jugular' of the U.S. Fuel Pipeline System Shuts Down after Cyberattack," *Politico*, May 8, 2021, https://www.politico.com/news/2021/05/08/colonial-pipeline-cyber-attack-485984.

CHAPTER 1: IF I HAD A TIME MACHINE

1. "Flying Blind in Third-Party Ecosystems," white paper, CybelAngel, https://cybelangel.com/third-party-ecosystem-landing-page/.

2. Amanda Fries, "Albany's Repair Cost after Ransomware Attack: $300,000," *Times Union*, September 27, 2019, https://www.timesunion.com/news/article/Ransomware-attack-on-Albany-cost-300K-to-14473544.php.
3. Manny Fernandez, David E. Sanger, and Marina Trahan Martinez, "Ransomware Attacks Are Testing Resolve of Cities Across America," *New York Times*, August 22, 2019, https://www.nytimes.com/2019/08/22/us/ransomware-attacks-hacking.html.
4. Lucas Ropek, "Louisiana Declares State Emergency After Malware Attack," *Government Technology*, July 25, 2019, https://www.govtech.com/security/Louisiana-Declares-State-Emergency-After-Malware-Attack-on-Multiple-School-Systems.html.
5. New York State Education Department, "2019 Data Privacy and Security Annual Report," http://www.nysed.gov/common/nysed/files/programs/data-privacy-security/annual-report-on-data-privacy-and-security-2019_0.pdf.
6. Emsisoft Malware Lab, "The State of Ransomware in the US: Report and Statistics 2020," Emsisoft blog, January 18, 2021, https://blog.emsisoft.com/en/37314/the-state-of-ransomware-in-the-us-report-and-statistics-2020/.

CHAPTER 2: FAIL TO PLAN OR PLAN TO FAIL: CYBER DISRUPTION RESPONSE PLANS AND CYBER INSURANCE

1. Michigan Cyber Range: https://en.wikipedia.org/wiki/Michigan_Cyber_Range; Dan Lohrmann, "The Michigan Cyber Range: Who, What, When, Where and How," *CSO Magazine*, November 15, 2012, https://www.csoonline.com/article/2135792/network-security-the-michigan-cyber-range-150-who-what-when-where-and-how.html; https://www.nga.org/wp-content/uploads/2020/05/MiC3-Memo.pdf; Rachel Cohen, "A Civilian Cybersecurity Reserve Corps Is Needed for the Pentagon and DHS, Lawmakers from Both Parties Say," *Air Force Times*, April 28, 2021, https://www.airforcetimes.com/news/your-air-force/2021/04/28/a-civilian-cybersecurity-reserve-corps-is-needed-for-the-pentagon-and-dhs-lawmakers-from-both-parties-say/.
2. Michigan Cyber Disruption Response Strategy of 2013: https://www.michigan.gov/documents/cybersecurity/Michigan_Cyber_Disruption_Response_Strategy_1.0_438703_7.pdf.
3. Michigan Cyber Disruption Response Plan of 2015: https://www.michigan.gov/documents/cybersecurity/120815_Michigan_Cyber_Disruption_Response_Plan_Online_VersionA_507848_7.pdf; see also Michigan Cyber Command Center (MC3) https://www.michigan.gov/msp/0,4643,7-123-72297_72370_72379_99838---,00.html.
4. Michigan Cyber Civilian Corps: https://www.michigan.gov/som/0,4669,7-192-78403_78404_78419---,00.html; Dan Lohrmann, "The Michigan Cyber Civilian Corps: Like a Volunteer Fire Department for Cybersecurity," *CSO Magazine*, June 9, 2014, https://www.csoonline.com/article/2360732/the-michigan-cyber-civilian-corps-like-a-volunteer-fire-department-for.html.

5. North American International Cyber Summit Series: https://www.michigan. gov/som/0,4669,7-192-78403_78404_78405-403764--,00.html; Dan Lohrmann, "Michigan Governor Snyder Releases New Cyber Initiative for Next Four Years," *Government Technology*, November 23, 2014, https://www.govtech.com/blogs/ lohrmann-on-cybersecurity/michigan-governor-snyder-releases-new-cyber-initiative-for-next-four-years.html.

6. FEMA Analysis of initial Michigan Cyber Disruption Response Strategy: https:// cip.gmu.edu/wp-content/uploads/2015/11/nps73-090514-05.pdf.

7. CISA Case Study Examining Michigan Cybersecurity Governance Model: https:// www.cisa.gov/sites/default/files/publications/Michigan_Cyber_Governance_ Case_Study_508.pdf.

8. Michigan Cyber Initiative, 2011 version: https://www.michigan.gov/documents/ cybersecurity/MichiganCyberInitiative2011_365631_7.pdf.

9. For more on CSO Kitchen Cabinet meetings, see Dan Lohrmann, "Top Five Mistakes New IT Security Leaders Make," *Government Technology*, November 24, 2013, https://www.govtech.com/blogs/lohrmann-on-cybersecurity/top-five-mistakes-new-it-security-leaders-make.html.

10. Dan Lohrmann, "A New Call to Action – Backstage at the Michigan Cyber Summit," *Government Technology*, October 8, 2011, https://www.govtech.com/blogs/ lohrmann-on-cybersecurity/a-new-call-to-100811.html.

11. "Secretary Napolitano Kicks Off National Cyber Security Awareness Month at Michigan Cyber Summit," Department of Homeland Security, press release, October 7, 2011, https://www.dhs.gov/news/2011/10/07/secretary-napolitano-kicks-national-cyber-security-awareness-month-michigan-cyber.

12. Lohrmann, "A New Call to Action."

13. Michigan Cyber Disruption Response Strategy of 2013: https://www.michigan. gov/documents/cybersecurity/Michigan_Cyber_Disruption_Response_Strat-egy_1.0_438703_7.pdf.

14. FEMA Lessons Learned on Information Sharing Covering the Michigan Cyber Disruption Response Strategy: https://cip.gmu.edu/wp-content/uploads/2015/11/ nps73-090514-05.pdf.

15. The National Association of State Chief Information Officers (NASCIO) Cyber Disruption Response Planning Guide: https://www.nascio.org/resource-center/ resources/cyber-disruption-response-planning-guide/.

16. National Governors Association (NGA) Issue Brief on State Cyber Disruption Response Plans: https://www.nga.org/wp-content/uploads/2019/04/Issue-Brief_MG.pdf.

17. NIST Special Publication 800-61 revision 2: https://nvlpubs.nist.gov/nistpubs/Spe-cialPublications/NIST.SP.800-61r2.pdf.

18. Development of NIST Cybersecurity Framework: https://www.nist.gov/cyber-framework/online-learning/history-and-creation-framework and https://www .nist.gov/cyberframework.

19. Comparison Guide between NIST and SANS incident response processes: https://cybersecurity.att.com/blogs/security-essentials/incident-response-steps-comparison-guide.

20. State-specific data breach reporting laws as listed by the National Conference of State Legislatures: https://www.ncsl.org/research/telecommunications-and-information-technology/security-breach-notification-laws.aspx.
21. List of incident response teams participating in FIRST, the Forum of Incident Response and Security Teams: https://www.first.org/members/teams/.
22. GOsafeonline in Singapore incident response checklist: https://www.csa.gov.sg/gosafeonline/resources/incident-response-checklist?s=09.
23. Crest Security Incident Response Guide – Version 1: https://www.crest-approved.org/wp-content/uploads/2014/11/CSIR-Procurement-Guide.pdf.
24. Cynet Incident Response Plan Templates and Guide: https://www.cynet.com/incident-response/incident-response-plan-template/.
25. Sam Friedman and Adam Thomas, "Demystifying Cyber Insurance Coverage," Deloitte University Press, 2017, https://www2.deloitte.com/content/dam/Deloitte/nl/Documents/financial-services/deloitte-nl-fsi-demystifying-cyber-insurance-coverage-report.pdf.
26. NGA, "States Confront the Cyber Challenge: Cyber Liability Insurance for States," https://www.nga.org/wp-content/uploads/2019/09/Cybersecurity-Insurance-Two-Pager-Final.pdf.

CHAPTER 3: PRACTICE MAKES PERFECT: EXERCISES, CYBER RANGES, AND BCPS

1. James Rundle, "NATO Wargame Examines Cyber Risk to Financial System," *Wall Street Journal*, April 15, 2021, https://www.wsj.com/articles/nato-wargame-examines-cyber-risk-to-financial-system-11618479000.
2. "Cybersecurity Exercise: Quantum Dawn V," SIFMA, https://www.sifma.org/resources/general/cybersecurity-exercise-quantum-dawn-v/.
3. SIFMA website organization description: https://www.sifma.org/.
4. "Financial Sector's Cybersecurity Global Readiness Exercised by Quantum Dawn V," SIFMA press release, February 27, 2020, https://www.sifma.org/resources/news/financial-sectors-cybersecurity-global-readiness-exercised-by-quantum-dawn-v/.
5. "DHS Strategic Action Plan to Counter the Threat Posed by the People's Republic of China: Defending the Homeland in the Era of Great Power Competition," U.S. Department of Homeland Security, January 14, 2021, https://www.waterisac.org/system/files/articles/21_0112_plcy_dhs-china-sap.pdf.
6. Blog post on Cyber Storm Exercises by Jeanette Manfra, the former Assistant Director for Cybersecurity for the Department of Homeland Security's Cybersecurity and Infrastructure Security Agency (CISA): "Cyber Storm VI: Testing the Nation's Ability to Respond to a Cyber Incident," April 13, 2018,https://www.dhs.gov/blog/2018/04/13/cyber-storm-vi-testing-nation-s-ability-respond-cyber-incident.
7. CISA Cyber Storm Exercise Final reports: https://www.cisa.gov/publication/cyber-storm-final-reports.

8. Dan Lohrmann, "CyberStorm II Panel Discusses Key Takeaways at RSA Conference," *CSO Magazine*, April 2008, https://www.csoonline.com/article/2135713/cyberstorm-ii-panel-discusses-key-takeaways-at-rsa-conference.html.

9. Cyber Exercise Playbook, November 2014, https://www.mitre.org/sites/default/files/publications/pr_14-3929-cyber-exercise-playbook.pdf.

10. CISA Exercise support website: https://www.cisa.gov/national-cyber-exercise-and-planning-program.

11. Center for Internet Security's six free tabletop exercises, https://www.cisecurity.org/white-papers/six-tabletop-exercises-prepare-cybersecurity-team/.

12. Virginia Cyber Range: https://www.virginiacyberrange.org/.

13. Michigan Cyber Range: https://en.wikipedia.org/wiki/Michigan_Cyber_Range and https://www.merit.edu/security/training/hubs/.

14. Palo Alto Networks Cyber Range: https://www.paloaltonetworks.com/solutions/initiatives/cyberrange-overview.

15. IBM Cyber Range: https://www.ibm.com/security/services/managed-security-services/command-center-mobile.

16. U.S. Cyber Range at Virginia Tech: https://www.uscyberrange.org/.

17. Dan Lohrmann, "Introducing the Michigan Cyber Range," *Government Technology*, November 12, 2012, https://www.govtech.com/blogs/lohrmann-on-cybersecurity/introducing-the-michigan-cyber-111212.html.

18. Merit description of Alphaville and Griffinville inside Michigan Cyber Range: https://www.merit.edu/security/training/alphaville/.

19. Cyber Risk Meetup, "Meet NASA Jet Propulsion Lab's CISO | The Mega C-Suite Stories EP 9", July 1, 2021, https://youtu.be/6ytqv6TwSJM.

CHAPTER 4: WHAT A LEADER NEEDS TO DO AT THE TOP

1. "Mega C-Suite Episode 7 with the World's First CISO," Steve Katz and host Shamane Tan, July 10, 2020, https://www.youtube.com/watch?v=e9b81LWodN4.

2. Cyber Risk Meetup, "Blackout Series – Leadership in Crisis with Brigadier General Gregory Touhill," December 12, 2020, https://youtu.be/CQZyf9Iu7rw.

3. Cyber Risk Meetup community: www.cyberriskmeetup.com.

4. Strategies to Mitigate Cyber Security Incidents, Australia Signals Directorate: https://www.cyber.gov.au/sites/default/files/2019-03/Mitigation_Strategies_2017.pdf.

5. https://www.cyber.gov.au/acsc/view-all-content/publications/essential-eight-maturity-model

6. The CISO Stress Report, Nominet Cyber Security: https://media.nominetcyber.com/wp-content/uploads/2020/02/Nominet_The-CISO-Stress-Report_2020_V10.pdf.

7. Shamane Tan, TEDx presentation, "The Imposter Syndrome of the Tall Poppies," May 6, 2020, https://www.youtube.com/watch?v=y6V9mOa_Sbs.

CHAPTER 5: WHERE WERE YOU WHEN THE SIRENS WENT OFF?

1. "A Closer Look at the DarkSide Ransomware Gang," Krebs on Security, May 11, 2021, https://krebsonsecurity.com/2021/05/a-closer-look-at-the-darkside-ransomware-gang/.
2. Mega C-Suite Stories podcast, "Leadership in Times of Crisis: Safety VS. Speed with the CIO at Toll Group – EP 15," September 2020, https://open.spotify.com/episode/5mj9IgImCnSdE5G4lR2DBz?si=5Gwh4hQoR3ubQtySaaCY1Q.

CHAPTER 6: WHERE DO WE GO WHEN THE POWER GOES OFF?

1. Kevin Poulsen, "Did Hackers Cause the 2003 Northeast Blackout? Umm, No," *Wired*, May 29, 2008, https://www.wired.com/2008/05/did-hackers-cau/.
2. Benjamin Freed, "How Texas Used Its Disaster Playbook after a Huge Ransomware Attack," *StateScoop*, October 15, 2019, https://statescoop.com/texas-ransomware-emergency-declaration-nascio-19/.
3. Texas SOC website: https://tdem.texas.gov/state-operations-center-soc/.
4. Colin Wood, "North Dakota's Building a Cybersecurity Operations Center – and Everyone's Invited," *StateScoop*, December 30, 2019, https://statescoop.com/north-dakotas-building-a-cybersecurity-operations-center-and-everyones-invited/.
5. Julia Edinger, "North Dakota Takes Multipronged Approach to Cybersecurity," *Government Technology*, April 5, 2021, https://www.govtech.com/security/north-dakota-takes-multipronged-approach-to-cybersecurity.html; Lucas Ropek, "North Dakota Expands Cyberdefense with New Funding, Workforce," *Government Technology*, November 13, 2019, https://www.govtech.com/security/north-dakota-expands-cyberdefense-with-new-funding-workforce.html.

CHAPTER 7: TEAMWORK IN THE MIDST OF THE FIRE

1. Dan Lohrmann, "Learning from the Best: James Collins, CIO of Delaware," *Government Technology*, September 5, 2020, https://www.govtech.com/blogs/lohrmann-on-cybersecurity/learning-from-the-best-james-collins-cio-in-delaware.html.
2. Dan Lohrmann, "Phil Bertolini Set the Excellence Standard for County CIOs," *Government Technology*, September 14, 2019, https://www.govtech.com/blogs/lohrmann-on-cybersecurity/phil-bertolini-set-the-excellence-standard-for-county-cios.html.
3. Dan Lohrmann, "Corporate Best Practices in Security Awareness and Training Programs," *Government Technology*, January 20, 2019, https://www.govtech.com/blogs/lohrmann-on-cybersecurity/corporate-best-practices-in-security-awareness-and-training-programs.html.
4. Dan Lohrmann, "Missouri CISO Michael Roling Leaves a Legacy of Excellence in Government Cybersecurity Leadership" *Government Technology*, September 23,

2018, https://www.govtech.com/blogs/lohrmann-on-cybersecurity/missouri-ciso-michael-roling-leaves-a-legacy-of-excellence-in-government-cybersecurity-leadership.html.

5. Jim Collins, "Good to Great," *Fast Company*, October 2001, https://www.jimcollins.com/article_topics/articles/good-to-great.html.

6. Encyclopedia of Management, "Zero-Based Budgeting," Reference for Business, https://www.referenceforbusiness.com/management/Tr-Z/Zero-Based-Budgeting.html.

CHAPTER 8: WHAT WENT RIGHT?

1. Cyber Risk Meetup, "Blackout Series – Leadership in Crisis with Brigadier General Gregory Touhill," December 12, 2020, https://youtu.be/CQZyf9Iu7rw.

2. Kevin Kok-Yew Tan, Augustine Pang, and Janelle Xiaoting Kang, "Breaking Bad News with CONSOLE: Toward a Framework Integrating Medical Protocols with Crisis Communication," *Public Relations Review* 45, no. 1 (March 2019): 153–166, https://www.sciencedirect.com/science/article/abs/pii/S0363811117303697.

3. Jacob Brogan, "Equifax's Data Breach PR Statement, a Close Reading," *Slate*, September 8, 2017, https://slate.com/technology/2017/09/a-close-reading-of-equifaxs-statement-about-its-data-breach.html.

4. Dara Khosrowshahi, "2016 Data Security Incident," Uber Newsroom, November 21, 2017, https://www.uber.com/newsroom/2016-data-incident/.

5. Office of the Australian Information Commissioner, "DonateBlood.com.au data breach (Australian Red Cross Blood Service)," https://www.oaic.gov.au/privacy/privacy-decisions/investigation-reports/donateblood-com-au-data-breach-australian-red-cross-blood-service/.

6. HM Revenue & Customs, "MLR3C14000 – Appendix 3: The National Intelligence Model (5x5x5)," https://www.gov.uk/hmrc-internal-manuals/money-laundering-regulations-compliance/mlr3c14000#:~:text=It%20is%20sometimes%20known%20informally,has%20access%20to%20the%20information.

7. Maz Saleem, "Why Facts Were Worth Nothing in the de Menezes Case," *Counterfire*, Opinion, April 4, 2016, https://www.counterfire.org/articles/opinion/18265-why-facts-were-worth-nothing-in-the-de-menezes-case.

8. Peter Squires, "The Catalogue of Errors That Killed Jean Charles de Menezes," *The Conversation*, July 21, 2015, https://theconversation.com/the-catalogue-of-errors-that-killed-jean-charles-de-menezes-45011.

CHAPTER 9: THE ROAD TO RECOVERY

1. Kim Zetter and Huib Modderkolk, "Revealed: How a Secret Dutch Mole Aided the U.S.-Israeli Stuxnet Cyberattack on Iran," *Yahoo! News*, September 2, 2019, https://news.yahoo.com/revealed-how-a-secret-dutch-mole-aided-the-us-israeli-stuxnet-cyber-attack-on-iran-160026018.html.

2. David Kushner, "The Real Story of Stuxnet," *IEEE Spectrum*, February 26, 2018, https://spectrum.ieee.org/telecom/security/the-real-story-of-stuxnet.

3. Cyber Risk Meetup, "Blackout Series – Leadership in Crisis with Brigadier General Gregory Touhill," December 12, 2020, https://www.youtube.com/watch?v=CQZyf9Iu7rw.

4. Melissa Agnes, "The Crisis Ready Formula for Managing Controversies," https://melissaagnes.com/formula-for-managing-controversies/.

CHAPTER 10: WHAT WENT WRONG – HOW DID WE MISS IT?

1. Steve Jobs Quotes, https://economictimes.indiatimes.com/people/steve-jobs-14-most-inspiring-quotes/slideshow/48051323.cms.

2. Will Englund and Ellen Nakashima, "Panic Buying Strikes Southeastern United States as Shuttered Pipeline Resumes Operations," *Washington Post*, May 12, 2021 (updated May 19, 2021), https://www.washingtonpost.com/business/2021/05/12/gas-shortage-colonial-pipeline-live-updates/.

3. Patrick Howell O'Neill, "A Patient Has Died after Ransomware Hackers Hit a German Hospital," *MIT Technology Review*, September 18, 2020, https://www.technologyreview.com/2020/09/18/1008582/a-patient-has-died-after-ransomware-hackers-hit-a-german-hospital/.

4. President Biden's Executive Order on Improving the Nation's Cybersecurity, May 12, 2021, https://www.whitehouse.gov/briefing-room/presidential-actions/2021/05/12/executive-order-on-improving-the-nations-cybersecurity/.

5. Robert McMillan and Dustin Volz, "Colonial Pipeline Hacker DarkSide Says It Will Shut Operations," *Wall Street Journal*, May 15, 2021, https://www.wsj.com/articles/web-site-of-darkside-hacking-group-linked-to-colonial-pipeline-attack-is-down-11621001688.

6. Critical infrastructure sectors website: https://www.cisa.gov/critical-infrastructure-sectors.

7. Thomas Brewster, "How Hackers Broke Equifax: Exploiting A Patchable Vulnerability," *Forbes*, September 14, 2017, https://www.forbes.com/sites/thomasbrewster/2017/09/14/equifax-hack-the-result-of-patched-vulnerability/?sh=13f5b7065cda.

8. Thomas Franck, "Equifax Used the Word 'admin' for the Login and Password of a Database," CNBC, September 14, 2017, https://www.cnbc.com/2017/09/14/equifax-used-admin-for-the-login-and-password-of-a-non-us-database.html.

9. Alia Shoaib, "Deloitte Cyber-Attack: Is Your Firm Safe?" *AccountancyAge*, September 26, 2017, https://www.accountancyage.com/2017/09/26/deloitte-cyber-attack-firm-safe/.

10. See mentoring examples: Thomas Lohrmann, "Security Pros Need a Mentor: Here's Why and How," *Government Technology*, February 9, 2018, https://www.govtech.com/blogs/lohrmann-on-cybersecurity/security-pros-need-a-mentor-heres-why-and-how.html.

11. Shamane Tan, *Cyber Risk Leaders: Global C-Suite Insights – Leadership & Influence in the Cyber Age*, My Security Media Pty, http://www.mysecuritymarketplace.com/crl/.

CHAPTER 11: TURNING CYBER INCIDENT LEMONS INTO ORGANIZATIONAL LEMONADE

1. "Cyber-Attack on Irish Health Service 'Catastrophic,'" BBC News, May 20, 2021, https://www.bbc.com/news/world-europe-57184977.
2. Joe Tidy, "Irish Cyber-Attack: Hackers Bail Out Irish Health Service for Free," BBC News, May 21, 2021, https://www.bbc.com/news/world-europe-57197688.
3. Sam Sabin, "Who's Next on Ransomware's Hit List," *Politico*, May 17, 2021, https://www.politico.com/newsletters/weekly-cybersecurity/2021/05/17/whos-next-on-ransomwares-hit-list-795343.
4. Carnegie Mellon Computer Security Incident Response Plan: https://www.cmu.edu/iso/governance/procedures/docs/incidentresponseplan1.0.pdf.
5. Jérôme Barthélemy, "Why Best Practices Often Fall Short," *MIT Sloan Management Review*, February 27, 2018, https://sloanreview.mit.edu/article/why-best-practices-often-fall-short/.
6. Pamela Hinds, "Research: Why Best Practices Don't Translate Across Cultures," *Harvard Business Review*, June 27, 2016, https://hbr.org/2016/06/research-why-best-practices-dont-translate-across-cultures.
7. Kacy Zurkus, "Clearing the Hurdles: Why Companies Have Not Implemented Basic Best Practices for Mobile Security," *Security Intelligence*, April 3, 2018, https://securityintelligence.com/clearing-the-hurdles-why-companies-have-not-implemented-basic-best-practices-for-mobile-security/.
8. John Belden, "Top 10 Excuses to Not Implement Best Practices and 5 Things to Do about It," *CIO Magazine*, July 24, 2017, https://www.cio.com/article/3209914/top-10-excuses-to-not-implement-best-practices-and-5-things-to-do-about-it.html.
9. Allen Gwinn, "Our Cybersecurity 'Industry Best Practices' Keep Allowing Breaches," *The Hill*, May 17, 2021, https://thehill-com.cdn.ampproject.org/c/s/thehill.com/opinion/technology/553891-our-cybersecurity-industry-best-practices-keep-allowing-breaches?amp.
10. Robert Carnevale, "Colonial Pipeline Ransomware Attack Linked to Microsoft Exchange Vulnerabilities," *Windows Central*, May 12, 2021 https://www.windowscentral.com/colonial-pipeline-ransomware-attack-linked-microsoft-exchange-vulnerabilities.
11. RSAC Conference USA 2021, virtual sessions on resilience and lessons learned in cybersecurity during the pandemic, "The RSAC Community Shares Their Stories of Resilience," https://www.youtube.com/watch?v=_twpsC-IJf0.
12. "Chloé Messdaghi Shares Her Story of Resilience, the RSAC 2021 Theme," https://www.youtube.com/watch?v=0kdr_rJNk18.

13. Anne Neuberger, Deputy National Security Advisor for Cyber and Emerging Technology, "Cybersecurity as a National Imperative," –RSAC 2021 Keynote, https://www.youtube.com/watch?v=KiOXZEgksXg.
14. Edward Segal, "7 Crisis Management Lessons from Colonial Pipeline's Response To Cyber Attack," *Forbes*, May 8, 2021, https://www.forbes.com/sites/edward-segal/2021/05/08/colonial-pipeline-cyber-attack-is-providing-crisis-management-lessons-in-real-time/?sh=405b824b3d82.
15. Paul Mee and Chaitra Chandrasekhar, "Cybersecurity Is Too Big a Job for Governments or Business to Handle Alone," World Economic Forum, May 3, 2021, https://www.weforum.org/agenda/2021/05/cybersecurity-governments-business/.
16. "National Cyber Incident Response Plan," U.S. Department of Homeland Security, December 2016, https://us-cert.cisa.gov/sites/default/files/ncirp/National_Cyber_Incident_Response_Plan.pdf.
17. About the NCSC, "Incident Management," National Cyber Security Centre, https://www.ncsc.gov.uk/section/about-ncsc/incident-management.
18. "Life's A Breach Report: Making Lemonade Out of Lemons," ISSA Conference, April 23, 2013, https://cdn.ymaws.com/www.members.issa.org/resource/resmgr/2013_april_web_conference_slides/2013_april_web_conference_-_.pdf.
19. NIST Cybersecurity Framework, "The Five Functions," https://www.nist.gov/cyberframework/online-learning/five-functions.
20. Tim Grance, Tamara Nolan, Kristin Burke, Rich Dudley, Gregory White, and Travis Good, "Guide to Test, Training, and Exercise Programs for IT Plans and Capabilities: Recommendations of the National Institute of Standards and Technology," NIST Special Publication 800-84, September 2006, pp. 5–6, https://nvlpubs.nist.gov/nistpubs/Legacy/SP/nistspecialpublication800-84.pdf.
21. Steve Morgan, "Global Cybercrime Damages Predicted to Reach $6 Trillion Annually by 2021," *Cybercrime Magazine*, October 26, 2020, https://cybersecurityventures.com/annual-cybercrime-report-2020/.
22. Steve Morgan, "Cybercrime to Cost the World $10.5 Trillion Annually by 2025," *Cybercrime Magazine*, November 13, 2020, https://cybersecurityventures.com/cybercrime-damage-costs-10-trillion-by-2025/.
23. Nick G., "How Many IoT Devices Are There in 2021? [All You Need To Know]," *Tech Jury*, last updated March 29, 2021, https://techjury.net/blog/how-many-iot-devices-are-there/.
24. Cyber Risk Meetup, "Meet Interpol's A/Director of Cybercrime Threat Response on The Mega C-Suite Stories," June 14, 2021, https://youtu.be/X1kfardpczw.

Index